Hartshorne
A New World View

Essays by Charles Hartshorne

Edited by

Herbert F. Vetter

Harvard Square Library
www.harvardsquarelibrary.org

Designed by Andrew Drane

Hartshorne: A New World View

Published by Harvard Square Library
www.harvardsquarelibrary.org

ISBN: 978-0-6151-4820-5

CONTENTS

Charles Hartshorne

INTRODUCTION

My work as a Harvard chaplain for 20 years was nourished by the new world view of Charles Hartshorne, a Harvard educated philosopher and scientist described by *Encyclopædia Britannica* as "the most influential proponent of a 'process philosophy' which considers God a participant in cosmic evolution."

Charles no sooner left the United States Army after World War I than he was promptly awarded, year after year, three Harvard University degrees: A.B. 1921, M.A. 1922, Ph.D. 1923. Today's graduate students may be surprised to learn that he wrote his 300 page doctoral dissertation, *The Unity of Being*, in 35 days. That ability to focus may help to explain his legendary absent-mindedness.

A favorite anecdote has him finishing a sidewalk chat with a student at a point midway between his home and his University of Chicago office, and asking, perplexedly, "Do you remember which way I was heading?" After two years of Harvard-funded travel as a Sheldon Fellow in Germany, France, and England, he was appointed an instructor in philosophy, with responsibility for teaching a course as well as assisting Alfred North Whitehead and tackling one other project. The department assigned him the appalling task of putting in order the roomful of boxes of jumbled manuscripts comprising the intellectual estate of Charles Sanders Peirce, the impoverished founder of this country's most distinguished philosophy, pragmatism, a mode of thought which has amply enriched our twentieth century world, but not its founder. The result was a Harvard University Press six volume set of *The Papers of Charles Sanders Peirce*, publicly revealing in 1931 and 1932 why both William James and Josiah Royce regarded Peirce as "America's Greatest Mind" to date. Hartshorne himself is now much more than a distinguished footnote to Peirce. Volume XX of *The Library of Living Philosophers* is entitled *The Philosophy of Charles Hartshorne*, putting him in the company of Albert Einstein, John Dewey, Bertrand Russell, Jean-

Paul Sartre, Martin Buber, and fellow Harvardians Whitehead, Santayana, and Quine. When I congratulated Charles upon the Library's selection of him for its pantheon of philosophers, he exclaimed with a smile, "The secret of my success is longevity." A truer secret of Hartshorne's success may well be that he is an exemplar of a great new tradition created by a group which I call the Harvard Square philosophers. Charles Sanders Peirce, William James, Alfred North Whitehead, William Ernest Hocking, and Charles Hartshorne share a unique vision of reality as social process. Perhaps some day scholars of the history of human thought will celebrate the universal wisdom displayed by their joint discovery. What the Harvard Square philosophers have been creating is a new worldview, a new synthesis of knowledge far surpassing the medieval synthesis of Thomism and the modern synthesis achieved by Spinoza. Here God is viewed not as a supernatural force breaking abruptly into history; God is the cosmic life of which our lives are a part. God is both humanity's endless source of joy and the cosmic sufferer who shares our pain. When we die, there is no endless heaven or hell to which we are consigned: the contribution which our lives have made continues in the ongoing deathless divine life. In this new cosmology, all creatures have some measure of free choice. Freedom is pervasive throughout the universe at all levels of reality. The future is always, to some extent, open. Creativity is the very essence of our well-ordered world and our everyday experience. Hartshorne's contributions to this synthesis include what the *Encyclopædia Britannica* calls "the definitive analysis" of panentheism (literally meaning "all in God"). For Hartshorne, "God includes the world even as an organism includes its cells, thus including the present moment of each event. The total organism gains from its constituents, even though the cells function with an appropriate degree of autonomy within the larger organism." The work of Hartshorne, whom I consider the Einstein of religious thought, is esteemed not only by some eminent secular scientists and philosophers but also by distinguished thinkers who are Protestant, Catholic, Jewish, Muslim, Hindu, and Buddhist. Nor is high esteem restricted to purely theoretical considerations divorced from urgent issues of life. Quincy Wright suggested in his classic two volume *A Study of War*

(1942) that Hartshorne's new philosophy of nature, described as theistic naturalism or naturalistic theism, is the type of religion needed for a peaceful world civilization "if only humanity becomes less reluctant to accept the new and abandon the old than it has been in the past." Various recent scholars have declared that no philosopher has devoted himself as profoundly as has Hartshorne to the concepts involved in the ecological crisis and that his work has important implications for bioethics. T. L. S. Sprigge at the University of Edinburgh offers a historical perspective: "Hartshorne has developed a metaphysical system which breaks fundamentally new ground. He has added to the great alternative systems of the universe." Other scholars praise him for his breadth—he has been described as one of the few great philosophers in Western history who have discussed and debated with Eastern systems and ideas as philosophy. Still others are astounded by his energy and his contribution to both philosophy and natural science. "What other nonagenarians have maintained his level of philosophical production?" asks Lewis Edwin Hahn, editor of the *Library of Living Philosophers*, referring to Hartshorne's contribution to the philosophy of creativity as well as mentioning his avocation—he enjoys an international reputation as an ornithologist, being an expert on bird song. Hartshorne's life was changed when, at the age of 16, he bought a pocket-sized songbird guide and a three power field glass. Over the years of his world travels related both to his teaching and his bird song research in Europe, Australia, India and Japan, he became an authority on this form of music which is second only to that of human members of the animal kingdom. The philosopher discovered that birds sing not only to win mates and protect territory but also to avoid monotony and to experience the sheer pleasure of singing. They sometimes vary their songs for hours on end. According to his research calibrations, some species actually sing not just one song but fifty or more songs or phrases. Hartshorne himself would like to be remembered as a writer. He is the author of twenty books and more than 500 papers. "I have written for later generations," he observes. "I might have done better to publish less, but one thing I cannot regret is taking as much time and energy from philosophy as was required to make my ornithological book, *Born to Sing: An Interpretation and Survey of World Bird Song*, possible."

When I spoke with him at his home in Austin, where he retired after long tenure at the University of Texas, Charles said that he suspects that he is the first person since Aristotle to interpret philosophy in relation to ornithology. I once asked Dorothy, her husband's superb editor over the years, to summarize the gist of his philosophy. "Love," she said, "is the guiding principle of all life. . . . All living organisms have at least an infinitesimal amount of freedom and responsibility. . . . We can consider a human life as being like a story, with a beginning, a middle, and an end. When we close the book, the story does not disappear. It continues, and likewise our contribution to others becomes a part of God's life that goes on and on." Many other details about the life and work of this person I admire are available in the Hartshorne Archives at the Center for Process Studies in Claremont, California. On one sheet of paper there, the eminent geneticist, Sewall Wright, drew the genealogy of Charles's mother's family—extending backward to Elder Brewster of the Pilgrims at Plymouth. When I found that historic genealogical detail in the Hartshorne Archive in Claremont, I also found hundreds of copies of his published articles which I had never seen before. My purpose in this presentation of his classic essays is to share some of this treasured wisdom with others who are eager to explore this new world view when it is presented in accessible form which does not require technical expertise in contemporary philosophy. Here then is a portion of the wisdom of Charles Hartshorne presented in his own words.

For encouragement of publication of this book I am indebted to the Hartshorne's daughter, Emily Schwartz, and to the three helpful professors of philosophy whom she suggested as advisors concerning this project: William L. Reese of the State University of New York, and author of the classic *Dictionary of Philosophy of Religion: Eastern and Western Thought*; Vincent Luizi, a judge and lawyer as well as chair of the Department of Philosophy at Southwest Texas State University, and author of *A Case for Legal Ethics*; and Randall E. Auxier, Professor of Philosophy at the University of Southern Illinois and editor of *The Library of Living Philosophy*, which includes *The Philosophy of Charles Hartshorne*.

H. F. V.
Cambridge, Massachusetts

Charles Hartshorne

ALBERT SCHWEITZER

"The greatest of all the spirit's task is to produce a worldview."

"The reconstruction of our age can begin only witha reconstruction of its theory of the universe. There is hardly anything more urgent in its claim on us than this which seems to be so far off and abstract."

-From *The Philosophy of Civilization* by Albert Schweitzer

Charles Hartshorne

ACKNOWLEDGMENTS

Grateful appreciation is expressed to the following sources for permission to publish the following articles:

"The Acceptance of Death," *Philosophical Aspects of Thanatology*, vol. 1, ed. Florence M. Hetzler and Austion H. Kutscher, New York: MSS Infomation Corporation, 1978.

"Religion and Creative Experience," *The Unitarian Register and the Universalist Leader*, June, 1952.

"Concerning Abortion," *Christian Century*, January 21, 1981.

"Theisitic Humanism," written in 1950 and here published for the first time.

"A New World and a New World View," the *Life of Choice*, ed. Clark Kucheman (Beacon Press, 1978)

"The Modern World and a Modern View of God," *Crane Review* 4, 2 (Winter, 1962).

"From Colonial Beginnings to Philosophical Greatness," *Monist* 48, 3 (July, 1964).

"The Idea of Creativity in American Philosophy," *The Journal of Karnatak University* (India), Social Sciences Vol. 2 (May, 1966).

"The Development of Process Philosophy," *Philosophers of Process*, ed. Douglas Browning (Random House, 1965).

"Can There Be Proofs for the Existence of God?" *Religious Language and Knowledge*, William T. Blackstone and Robert H. Ayers, The University of Georgia (Athens, 1972)

"Freedom, Individuality, and Beauty in Nature." *Snowy Egret* 24, 2 (Autumn, 1960)

Charles Hartshorne

THE ACCEPTANCE OF DEATH

Since all of us die, it is clear that the meaning of life must be inseparable from the meaning of death. If we cannot understand death, we cannot understand life, and vice versa. Life and death are two sides of one reality.

In principle life is good while it lasts. The meaning of life is, in part at least, the simple goodness of living. Normally we are glad to be alive. We may imagine circumstances in which we would be much more intensely glad to be alive than we actually are, but still life seems better than just no life. Even when things go badly with us, I think we deceive ourselves if we think that we derive no satisfaction from the activities of the living. The person who proclaims her or his misery derives some value merely from breathing and eating, some value from choosing the words in which the self is expressed, some value from making one's troubles an object of attention and observing the way other people react to them. I believe that living is essentially voluntary, and that no one can be compelled to exist, unless on a largely unconscious level. If the will to live really dies, then we are already virtually dead. The person who decides to commit suicide gets some satisfaction out of thinking, "now it will soon be over." This satisfaction is what keeps the person still among the living until performing some physical action which ends life, but then the bullet or poison, not directly the will to die, is what ends the life. Willing to live and finding life better than nothing are, I hold, the same things.

Take the person who stays alive because of fear of hell. Then what sustains the will to live is the thought, "I am better as I am than I might be in hell; I don't have to be in hell, at least not yet." Thinking thus gives present life some value. Or, if a mother lives for the sake

1

of her children, the interest in the children and approval of herself as living for them make it possible for her to achieve at least some mild satisfaction in her own activities.

Though living is always more or less voluntary, dying can be either with or without our choice, not only because, on the one hand, external forces in action ourselves, but also because we can will not to live beyond a certain point of time. Or at least, we can be entirely content with the thought of not living forever or much beyond some specified point in our individual careers. We can choose to stop trying particularly to live, accepting death as coming from old age or terminal illness; we can be on the side of the physical forces that tend toward our death.

There are three principal ways of trying to make death as such acceptable. We can believe, or try to believe, in personal immortality in the conventional sense, meaning that after death we are to become conscious again; somewhat as we do in waking from a deep sleep, but this time in some supernatural heaven or hell, or on some other planet or in some other animal body. This may or may not be with memory of our previous earthly career. In either case this is a view which cannot appeal to any definite well-documented or scientific evidence to support it. I think that the appeal of this view is largely a consequence of misconceptions about the nature of life as such, no matter where or when.

Another way of arguing that death is good, or at least not too bad, is that it is like going into a dreamless sleep and never waking up again. Thus, there is no suffering in being dead, though there may be in dying, and so we escape from the evils of life once and for all. Note, however, that only for the others, the spectators, can it be "better" that we are no longer suffering. The suicide who reasons, "I shall be better off dead" will not be better or worse off, not yet just the same: simply he or she will not be in any state whatsoever, good, bad, or neutral. Into no future will the person survive to benefit since the future after death will not be hers or his at all. The suicide must act whether for personal satisfaction in the moments before death, or else for the benefit of those who survive. My conclusion is that the comparison of death to dreamless sleep is not enough to show that death is a good thing for the individual who dies.

The third way of making death acceptable is that of transcending self-interest as our final concern. If, and only if, we can regard our entire lives as contributing to the good of those who will survive us and if we can find part of our present satisfaction in the thought of such contribution to the future of life beyond ourselves, can we find death positively acceptable. I call this doctrine "contributionism." It includes, but is more than, what is sometimes called "service" to others, for that is too much confined to things we do for others, actions from which others may benefit, like giving lectures. By "contributionism" I mean more than this. I mean that simply by being what we are in ourselves we contribute to the future of life. Our present happiness is a central factor in this contribution. Miserable people, even if they are useful, contribute less than happy people who are also useful. By giving posterity our misery to look back upon, we do them no special favor. It is joys one wants to recall, more than sufferings. Even admitting the truth in the poet's phrase, "our sweetest songs are those that tell of saddest thought," still, in the composing and singing of these songs, there is more than misery; there is satisfaction in the beauty of the expression of grief.

To accept death as ending our personal career is to regard that career as a finite or bounded thing. We are finite in space and time; indeed, we are mere fragments of reality spatially and temporally, but then any work of art or beautiful thing is such a fragment, apart from the entire universe throughout time. Contentment with mortality is contentment with the finitude of our ultimate contribution to the whole of life. Should our careers have a last episode? Should a book have a last chapter? A poem, a last verse? Without beginning and end a work of art has no definite form or meaning. I personally regard a life as, with normal luck and good management, having something of the qualities of a work of art, and I see no reason why it should be endless; rather the contrary, it ought not to be endless.

Part of the interest of life is that it has a beginning, a middle, and an end. There are dramatic contrasts between infancy and youth, youth and maturity, maturity and elderliness, and these contrasts are spanned by certain life purposes, finite in scope, that bind them together. What more does one wish? If going to sleep is nothing dreadful, why is it dreadful to think of a sleep without waking? For the sleeper the fact that he or she does not awaken is as nothing. Only the others experience the not waking up.

What bothers people is perhaps the idea that death is the mere absence of life, but my death is only the absence of my continued living, it is not the absence of all living. New lives make their finite contributions to the future of life as a whole.

If contributionism is to solve the problem of death, certain other ideas are required.

1. One must be able to see that for our present satisfaction in living it is not necessary to foresee everlasting future rewards to ourselves for our actions. The personal reward for living is essentially in the living itself. We live because we will to live, and this means that our essential reward is in the present.

2. What is necessary for present satisfaction is only some answer to the question, "What good will it be, after the present has gone into the past, that we have been happy, and why will it matter if we have been miserable, that is, far less happy than we might have been?" If happiness and misery are merely nullified by becoming past, then is not the last word about life that it signifies nothing and is destined to become indistinguishable from nothing? If we are not to be there benefiting from our having lived well rather than ill, still some life must be there which can be supposed to have benefited from our lives. What is called "social immortality," is at least a move in the required direction.

3. However, social immortality in the merely human sense is at the mercy of doubts about the future of the species, and also about the extent to which our now being happy or good may, or perhaps may not, make a significant contribution to that future. Supposing nuclear war, perhaps there will be nothing left to which the contribution can be made. No way is apparent to guarantee that humanity will always escape destruction of the species. Only if we can believe in a superhuman and in some strict sense divine form of life, to which our lives can make contributions proportional to their goodness or beauty, only then is the permanence of our contributions clearly implied. I hold that this solves the basic question about death, which is how the meaning of life can survive its termination.

4. It is one thing to have a view about the general fact that we all must die and another to know what to think about the endless variety of ways in which persons die, some in infancy, some in ripe old age, some in agony, some peacefully in their sleep, and so forth. I have two things to say about this: it is partly a matter of chance, and partly a matter of good or bad management. There are misfortunes that no wisdom and no effort by the individual could have guarded against; but also there are foolish or weak decisions or actions that greatly diminish one's chances of living out a normal life span. I have developed a philosophy according to which, in spite of a real framework of providential order in the world, the details of what happens in it are genuinely matters of chance. Not God, and not any creature, decides precisely what happens to you or me, but innumerable creatures together decide it, no one of them having any definite idea in advance of the happenings. God's role in the world is not in selecting details of creaturely careers, but in maintaining certain limits to the disorder and conflict that creatures can fall into as they make their own decisions.

I am deeply convinced that it is a religious mistake to ask, in case of misfortune, why did God do this to me? God is not in the business of inflicting misfortunes upon anyone. It is other creatures, for example bacteria, or human thieves or mischief-makers, that inflict misfortunes. God makes it possible for there to be a cosmic order in which creatures can live and make their own decisions. This order does make it inevitable that there will be some misfortunes, but the particular ones are not divinely, but creaturely chosen. Always many creatures together are involved. Thus, so far as any one creature's intentions go, it is a matter of chance that this or that happen to you or me.

Show me a philosopher or theologian who denies that chance is pervasive in life, and I will show you one who can give no acceptable view of the concrete facts of good and evil. If he or she believes in God, they can say nothing to the purpose about the theological problem of evil, and if they do not believe in God, then they are committed to a blind, amoral necessity that acts with the same shocking indifference to our suffering that theological determinism attributes to deity. Only chance intersections of many actions by many agents can acceptably account for evils.

Nontheological determinists are, in spite of themselves, committed to chance, for the entire cosmic system from which, according to them, every event is a necessary consequence, has itself no explanation and is as a whole like an immensely complex throw of the dice, with no intelligible account possible either of the dice or the dice thrower. Chance must be admitted somewhere, but the place to admit it is everywhere, just as some aspects of order are everywhere. Quantum physics shows in principle how the two can be combined. Given certain limits to randomness (which limits I view as providential) and large numbers of similar happenings, there will then be statistical regularities, and yet each single agent can be making its own little decision.

A contemporary philosopher has told us that we to well to be mindful of our own mortality. Long before I met him in 1924, I had given thought to this matter. It was one of the reasons, not the only one, for my reaching the firm conclusion, never afterward abandoned, that self-interest, no matter how "enlightened," is not the key to motivation. While we live, others may contribute to our happiness; but in the end happiness itself is nothing unless there be something for which it is important that this happiness occurred as it did, something which, having once acquired our earthly careers as parts of its own life and value, can never thereafter lose them. The "posterity" for which we finally live needs to be more than human, it needs to be a life which cherishes us and all creatures forever for the intrinsic beauty and joy we have actually achieved. While we live, others may serve us, but in death no one can be served. However, our having lived as we have can continue to serve others, at least that supreme "Other" able appreciate all the forms of value there can be, the supreme conductor of the universal symphony who is also its final and definitive auditor, to deserve whose infinitely discriminating applause is that for which, knowingly or otherwise, all our efforts are, as I believe, directed.

What do we get out of it all? We get the satisfaction of being able to find a rational meaning in our lives now while we live them. Heaven and hell are here and now. The ultimate future belongs, not to us, but to God and whatever new creatures may follow our decease and that of our friends and enemies.

Death is a riddle to which no mere egoist, no denier of chance, no one who fails to see that beauty and finitude belong together, and finally no one without some sense of the superhuman or cosmic, the truly immortal reality, can ever find the key. Transcendence of the primarily selfish way of seeing the future, rejection of the purely deterministic view of causality, acceptance of the aesthetic need for finitude, and faith that there is a superhuman and everlasting good which we, in our humble way, can enhance or enrich, this combination is the fourfold key to the riddle of life and death.

Charles Hartshorne

CONCERNING ABORTION: AN ATTEMPT AT A RATIONAL VIEW

My onetime colleague T. V. Smith once wrote a book called *Beyond Conscience*, in which he waxed eloquent in showing the harm that good people do. To live according to one's conscience may be a fine thing, but what if A's conscience leads A to try to compel B and C to live, not according to B's or C's conscience, but according to A's? That is what many opponents of abortion are trying to do. To propose a constitutional amendment to this effect is one of the most outrageous attempts to tyrannize over others that I can recall in my long lifetime as an American citizen. Proponents of the antiabortion amendment make their case, if possible, even worse when they defend themselves with the contention, "It isn't my conscience only—it is a commandment of religion." For now one particular form of religion is being used in an attempt to tyrannize over other forms of religious or philosophical belief. The separation of church and state evidently means little to such people.

IN WHAT SENSE HUMAN?

Ours is a country that has many diverse religious groups, and many people who cannot find truth in any organized religious body. It is a country that has great difficulty in effectively opposing forms of killing that everyone admits to be wrong. Those who would saddle the legal system with matters about which consciences sincerely and strongly differ show a disregard of the country's primary needs. The same is to be said about crusades to make things difficult for homosexuals. There can be little freedom if we lose sight of the vital distinction between moral questions and legal ones. The law compels and coerces, with the implicit threat of violence; morals seek to persuade. It is a poor society that forgets this difference.

What is the moral question regarding abortion? Some people say that the fetus is alive and that, therefore, killing it is wrong. Since mosquitoes, bacteria, apes and whales are also alive, the argument is less than clear. Even plants are alive. I am not impressed by the rebuttal, "But plants, mosquitoes, bacteria and whales are not human, and the fetus is." For the issue now becomes, in what sense is the fetus human? No one denies that its origin is human, as is its possible destiny, but the same is true of every unfertilized egg in the body of a nun. Is it wrong that some such eggs are not made or allowed to become human individuals?

Granted that a fetus is human in origin and possible destiny, in what further sense is it human? The entire problem lies here. If there are pro-life activists who have thrown much light on this question, I do not know their names. One theologian who writes on the subject—Paul Ramsey—thinks that a human egg cell becomes a human individual with a moral claim to survive if it has been fertilized. Yet this egg cell has none of the qualities that we have in mind when we proclaim our superior worth to the chimpanzees or dolphins. It cannot speak, reason or judge between right and wrong. It cannot have personal relations, without which a person is not functionally a person at all, until months—and not, except minimally, until years—have passed. Even then, it will not be a person in the normal sense unless some who are already fully persons have taken pains to help it become a human being in the full value sense, functioning as such. The antiabortionist is commanding some person or persons to undertake this effort. For without it, the fetus will never be human in the relevant sense. It will be human only in origin, but otherwise a subhuman animal.

The fertilized egg is an individual egg, but not an individual human being, for such a being is, in its body, a multicellular organism, a metazoan—to use the scientific Greek—and the egg is a single cell. The first thing the egg cell does is to begin dividing into many cells. During its first weeks there seems to be no ground for regarding the fetus as comparable to an individual animal. Only in possible or probable destiny is it an individual. Otherwise it is an organized society of single-celled individuals.

A possible individual person is one thing; an actual person is another. If this difference is not important, what is? There is in the long run no room in the solar system, or even in the known universe for all human eggs—even all fertilized eggs, as things now stand—to become human persons. Indeed, it is mathematically demonstrable that the present rate of population growth must be lowered somehow. There is no moral imperative that all possibilities of human persons become actual persons.

Of course, some may say that the fertilized egg already has a human soul, but on what evidence? The evidence of soul in the relevant sense is the capacity to reason, judge right and wrong, and the like.

GENETIC AND OTHER INFLUENCES

One may also say that since the fertilized egg has a combination of genes (the units of physical inheritance) from both parents, in this sense it is already a human individual. There are two objections, either one in my opinion conclusive but only one of which is taken into account by Ramsey. The one he does mention is that identical twins have the same gene combination. The theologian does not see this as decisive, but I do.

The other objection is that it amounts to a very crude form of materialism to identify individuality with the gene combination. Genes are the chemical bearers of inherited traits. This chemical basis of inheritance presumably influences everything about the development of the individual—influences, but does not fully determine. To say that the entire life of the person is determined by heredity is a theory of unfreedom that my religious conviction can only regard as monstrous, and there are biophysicists and neurophysiologists who agree with me.

From the gene-determined chemistry to a human person is a long, long step. As soon as the nervous system forming in the embryo begins to function as a whole—and not before—the cell colony begins to turn into a genuinely individual animal. One may reasonably suppose that this change is accompanied by some extremely primitive individual animal feelings. They cannot be recognizably human feelings, much less human thoughts, and cannot compare with the feeling of a porpoise or chimpanzee in level of consciousness. That much seems as certain as anything about the fetus except its origin and possible destiny. The nervous system of a very premature baby has been compared by an expert to that of a pig, and we know, if we know anything about this matter, that it is the nervous system that counts where individuality is concerned.

Identical twins are different individuals, each unique in consciousness. Though having the same genetic makeup, they will have been differently situated in the womb and hence will have received different stimuli. For that reason, if for no other, they will have developed differently, especially in their brains and nervous systems, but there are additional reasons for the difference in development. One is the role of chance, which takes many forms. We are passing through a great cultural change in which the idea, long dominant in science, that chance is "only a word for our ignorance of causes" is being replaced by the view that the real laws of nature are probabilistic and allow for aspects of genuine chance.

Another reason is that it is reasonable to admit a reverse influence of the developing life of feelings in the fetus on the nervous system, as well as of the system upon the feelings. Since I, along with some famous philosophers and scientists, believe in freedom (not solely of mature human beings but—in some slight degree—of all individuals in nature, down to the atoms and farther), I hold that even in the fetus the incipient individual is unconsciously making what on higher levels we call "decisions." These decisions influence the developing nervous system. Thus, to a certain extent we make our own bodies by our feelings and thoughts. An English poet with Platonic ideas expressed this concept as follows,

"The body from the soul its form doth take, for soul is form and doth the body make." The word soul is, for me, incidental. The point is that feelings, thoughts, experiences react on the body and partly mold its development.

THE RIGHTS OF PERSONS

Paul Ramsey argues (as does William Buckley in a letter to me) that if a fetus is not fully human, then neither is an infant. Of course an infant is not fully human. No one thinks it can, while an infant, be taught to speak, reason or judge right and wrong, but it is much closer to that stage than is a three-month fetus. It is beginning to have primitive social relations not open to a fetus; and since there is no sharp line anywhere between an infant and a child able to speak a few words, or between the latter and a child able to speak very many words, we have to regard the infant as significantly different from a three-month or four-month fetus. Nevertheless, I have little sympathy with the idea that infanticide is just another form of murder. Persons who are already functionally persons in the full sense have more important rights even than infants. Infanticide can be wrong without being fully comparable to the killing of persons in the full sense.

Does this distinction apply to the killing of a hopelessly senile person (or one in a permanent coma)? For me it does. I hope that no one will think that if, God forbid, I ever reach that stage, it must be for my sake that I should be treated with the respect due to normal human beings. Rather, it is for the sake of others that such respect may be imperative. Symbolically, one who has been a person may have to be treated as a person. There are difficulties and hazards in not so treating such individuals.

Religious people may argue that once a fetus starts to develop, it is for God, not human beings, to decide whether the fetus survives and how long it lives. This argument assumes, against all evidence, that human life spans are independent of human decisions. Our medical hygiene has radically altered the original "balance of nature." Hence the population explosion. Our technology makes pregnancy more and more a matter of human decision; more and more our choices are influencing the weal and woe of the animals on this earth. It is an awesome responsibility, but one that we cannot avoid. After all, the book of Genesis essentially predicted our dominion over terrestrial life. No one is proposing to make abortion compulsory for those morally opposed to it. I add that everyone who smokes is taking a hand in deciding how long he or she will live. Also everyone who, by failing to exercise reasonably, allows his or her heart to lose its vigor. Our destinies are not simply "acts of God."

I may be told that if I value my life I must be glad that I was not aborted in the fetus state. Yes, I am glad, but this expression does not constitute a claim to having already had a "right," against which no other right could prevail, to the life I have enjoyed. I feel no indignation or horror at contemplating the idea the world might have had to do without me. The world could have managed, and as for what I would have missed, there would have been no such "I" to miss it.

POTENTIAL, NOT ACTUAL

With almost everything they say, the fanatics against abortion show that they will not, or cannot, face the known facts of this matter. The inability of a fetus to say "I" is not merely a lack of skill; there is nothing there to which the pronoun could properly refer. A fetus is not a person but a potential person. The "life" to which "pro-life" refers is nonpersonal, by any criterion that makes sense to some of us. It is subpersonal animal life only. The mother, however, is a person.

I resent strongly the way many males tend to dictate to females their behavior, even though many females encourage them in this. Of course, the male parent of a fetus also has certain rights, but it remains true that the female parent is the one most directly and vitally concerned.

I shall not forget talking about this whole matter to a wonderful woman, the widow of a philosopher known for his idealism. She was doing social work with young women and had come to the conclusion that abortion is, in some cases, the lesser evil. She told me that her late husband had said, when she broached the subject to him, "but you can't do that." "My darling," she replied, "we are doing it." I see no reason to rate the consciences of the pro-lifers higher than this woman's conscience. She knew what the problem was for certain mothers. A society that flaunts sex in all the media makes it difficult for the young to avoid unwanted pregnancy, and it does little to help them with the most difficult of all problems of self-discipline. Some of us tell young persons that they are murderers if they resort to abortion, so we should not be surprised that Margaret Mead, that clear-sighted observer of our society and of other societies, should say, "Abortion is a nasty thing, but our society deserves it." Alas, it is too true.

I share something of the disgust of hard-core opponents of abortion that contraceptives, combined with the availability of abortion, may deprive sexual intercourse of spiritual meaning. The sacramental view of marriage has always had appeal to me, and my life has been lived accordingly. Abortion is indeed a nasty thing, but unfortunately there are in our society many even nastier things, like the fact that some children are growing up unwanted. This for my conscience is a great deal nastier, and truly horrible. An overcrowded world is also nasty, and could in a few decades become truly catastrophic.

The argument against abortion that the fetus may be a potential genius has to be balanced against the much more probable chance of its being a mediocrity, or a destructive enemy of society. Every egg cell is a possible genius and also a possible monster in human form. Where do we stop in calculating such possibilities?

If some who object to abortion work to diminish the number of unwanted, inappropriate pregnancies, or to make bearing a child for adoption by persons able to be its loving foster parents more attractive than it now is, and do this with a minimum of coercion, all honor to them. In view of the population problem, the first of these remedies should have high priority.

Above all, the coercive power of our legal system, already stretched thin, must be used with caution and chiefly against evils about which there is something like universal consensus. That persons have rights is a universal belief in our society, but that a fetus is already an actual person—about that there is and there can be no consensus. Coercion in such matters is tyranny. Alas for our dangerously fragmented and alienated society if we persist in such tyranny.

Charles Hartshorne

RELIGION AND CREATIVE EXPERIENCE

That man has a certain creative power is a commonplace nowadays. Making the most of this power is what is termed "living creatively." Not only is creativity a widely recognized ideal for human action, it is also the first principle of the most daring and powerful philosophical system of this century, that of Whitehead, and Whitehead was preceded in this by other less notable philosophers.

For these philosophers, to be is to create; it is impossible to exist at all in absolutely uncreative fashion. From atoms to deity, all things in their degree and kind act creatively. I believe that we have in this rather new type of philosophy an intellectual basis for religion far superior to any other. Unfortunately only a few, even among professional philosophers, have as yet a clear idea of this way of thinking.

First, what is it to create? Whitehead takes as his primary example the process of human experiencing. His doctrine is simple: to experience is to create. What is the resulting product? Experience itself. Each experience is something new and unique, and to experience is always a free production of novelty. Bergson had already said this, but Whitehead makes it the central category of an ambitious system.

People have looked for freedom in action, and of course freedom must somehow show up in action. Still, the first stage of free action is the way in which we interpret or experience the world. Only you or I can determine our own way of feeling and thinking our environment. The utmost slave has some freedom here which none can wholly suppress while the slave is alive. No matter how others coerce or persuade, he or she finally must make a unique and unpredictable response to the stimuli others bring to bear.

17

It is vain to talk about psychological prediction as an absolute; for even after an experience has taken place not all the words in all languages could precisely describe that experience; and what cannot be said even afterwards certainly cannot be said in advance. Suppose that a person grows angry, as we have predicted. There are as many forms and qualities of angry experience as there are cases, and only more or less rough and crude descriptions of their differences are possible.

Every experience is in some degree an unpredictable novelty. The stimuli molding an experience are many: the five or nine senses are operating; memory is relating us, at least unconsciously, to thousands of incidents of the past; but this multiplicity of influences is to produce a single unitary experience. The effect is one; the causes, however, are always many. This vast multitude of factors must flow together to produce a single new entity, the experience of the moment. By no magic can casual laws derive this new unity from the previous multiplicity. Certainly, the many stimuli tell us much about the response, but it is a logical impossibility that they should tell us all. An emergent synthesis is needed to decide just how each item is to blend in a single complex sensory-emotional-intellectual whole, the experience. Any motives are either but items going into the synthesis, or else they are the synthesis. To experience must be a free act, or nothing intelligible.

Why is this not more generally realized? In part, because we have our minds chiefly upon the more important and exceptional modes of creativity, and so we overlook the humbler ones which are always there, like the man in Moliere who did not realize that he had been talking "prose" all his life. Freedom is always there, but the unusual kinds and degrees of freedom are not always there. While it is indeed important to distinguish between the higher and lower forms of freedom, we shall never understand life and the world until we see that the zero degree of freedom can only be the zero of experiencing, and even of reality. Apart from experience the idea of reality is empty, as some though not all philosophers admit. Accordingly, Whitehead proposes that we generalize, and take the free act of experiencing as the universal principle of reality. Not that human experience is the principle of reality, far from it. Human experience is only one form; from humans to molecules and atoms, we have a series of modes of organization; at no point can one say, "Below this there could be no experience." If atoms respond to stimuli (and they do), how else could they show that they sense or feel? If you say that they have no sense organs, the reply is: neither do one-celled animals, yet they seem to perceive their environments.

Imagine the universe as a vast system of experiencing individuals on innumerable levels. Each individual is in some measure free, for experiencing is a partly free act. Thus creativity, emergent novelty, is universal. In this way we perhaps understand why the physicists have had to reformulate the laws of nature as statistical, and not absolute uniformities.

If all individuals act freely, what prevents the world from falling into hopeless confusion and chaos? How can there be even statistical regularities? Must not limits be somehow imposed upon freedom in order to make a world? How are the limits imposed?

There are but two possible answers in a philosophy of universal creative experience. Either the various forms of experience scattered through nature miraculously limit or control themselves and each other and thus preserve a measure of harmony or mutual compatibility; or else some superior or at least cosmic, form of freedom furnishes a "directive" which ordinary freedom accepts or obeys. Without guidance, order seems a mere mystery. In a philosophy of freedom, only a superior form of creativity, to which all things respond and whose influence is given a certain priority, can furnish the guidance which orders the world.

This is one way of putting the argument for belief in God. Divine action is supreme freedom furnishing a general direction to all lesser forms of freedom, thereby giving the universe an order.

How is this cosmic direction imparted? How does the divine creativity act on the lesser creativities? How do lesser creativities act on each other? The answer which the new type of philosophy gives is as follows. Experience must have stimuli. We do not experience in a vacuum, nor does one simply experience his own experience of his own experience—experience of what? There must be objects of experience, data which are already there, ready to be experienced. If nothing is in the world but creative experience, what then are the objects which are experienced? Simply, previous cases of experience? Some of these are one's own earlier experiences as one now remembers them. The rest are of other kinds.

The cells of one's body are, I believe, constantly furnishing their little experiences which, pooled together in our more comprehensive experience, constitute what we call our sensations. The cells respond to, or experience, our experiences, as is shown by the influence our thoughts and feelings have upon our bodily changes. The stimuli always influence the response, but they never wholly determine it. Recall also that the stimuli are really earlier responses, experiences which had their own stimuli. Thus, what sets limits to the freedom of a response is simply previous, partly free responses which have now become stimuli. When two of us talk, each response of one becomes a stimulus to the other. Always there is a degree of freedom; and the limit upon the present act of freedom is the sum of past acts to which it is a reaction. Experience as emergent synthesis feeds on its own previous products, and on nothing else whatever. This is the only intelligible escape from a blind dualism of mind and matter.

What prevents anarchy, if freedom alone limits freedom? Keeping to our language of stimulus and response, what is needed to order the world is a higher level of response, which like every form of response becomes in its turn a stimulus—in this case, the supreme stimulus. Each individual in the world is in dialogue with its neighbors, influencing and being influenced by them; but each individual is also and above all in dialogue, largely unconscious no doubt, with the divine individual.

Is this not the traditional belief in God, in new verbal dress? It is, and it isn't. The old view had some disturbing features, which our language avoids. It was usually said that while God influenced all things, nothing influenced God. For God there are no stimuli; hence when divine power influences or stimulates the world, it is in a wholly extraordinary way. God, in the old theory, does not respond, but merely creates, "out of nothing." If we refuse to allow an analogy between ordinary creative action and the divine "creating" of the cosmos, we use a word the meaning of which we cannot provide. Our new philosophical doctrine is that even God's creativity is a higher form of emergent synthesis, or response to stimuli. God influences us supremely because God is supremely open to our influence and responds infinitely delicately to all things, while we respond delicately only to changes in our brain cells. God contributes to our lives in superior fashion in equally superior fashion, of receiving contributions from us. Like the sensitive parent or ruler, God enjoys observing our feelings and thoughts and responds to them with a perfection of appreciation to which no parent or ruler can attain. Because only God can appreciate us, together with all our neighbors, in our full worth, we unconsciously respond to this appreciation as we do not to any other, and so the order of the world is possible despite the assumption that only freedom exists to limit freedom.

Consider now the advantages of this way of viewing God. Unlike the notion of divine creation as a purely one way action proceeding from God, our view does not threaten to deny the freedom or creativity of the creatures. How many theologians have talked as though God, being supremely free, produced individuals wholly without freedom? Individuals think they make decisions, but God, we say, has made all things, hence all decisions, but if God has literally and completely "made" my decision, how is it mine? Granted that we are willing to think of ourselves as absolute puppets whose every move is wholly controlled by deity, how could such puppets even have the notion of freedom form the theory that they are puppets controlled by the free decisions of God? Or would God, for them, be the great puppet—controlled by what? The entire view seems logically untenable. In our philosophy of universal freedom, no such divine monopoly upon decision making can be conceived. To create is to respond to the creative freedom of others; hence to be supremely creative is to respond supremely to that freedom.

Look at another difference between the usual theistic doctrine and our view. If God creates by sheer fiat, out of nothing, why does God not make a world wholly good? I suggest that the very problem is false. We do not need to worship any such all-determining creator in God. Of course, a worshipful God must have the supreme cosmic, or perfect, form of creative power. To say that in God is the perfect or infinite form of creative response to the freedom of others is to imply that God has the freedom of others to respond to. Why, then is there evil in the world? Because the making of the world is not a simple act of deity, but a fusion of divine and lesser acts, all in their fashion self-determining, creative or free.

As Lequier said, a century ago, God has created us creators of ourselves. Does such a view "limit" the power of God? This way of putting the question prejudices the answer and is to be rejected. To exert power, in our view, is to respond to the responses of others in such a way that the new response becomes in its turn a new stimulus. In this philosophy the word power has no other meaning which could be used to describe God. So we need not limit God's power to make room for the freedom of the creatures or to explain evil; we need only take care that when we speak of divine or perfect "power," we have a meaning for the word.

This meaning will take care of creaturely freedom automatically. If all creatures must be free, then no divine directive could do more than set boundaries to the possibilities of discord and disorder in the world. Absolute order could in no way be guaranteed, not because God is weak, but because it would not be strength to abolish creaturely freedom and with it any world upon which the strength could be exercised. The problem of evil in its classical form is a pseudoproblem, due to the misuse of words. Millions of people over the earth do not believe in God, they would tell you, chiefly because of evil. The book of Job hints at my position.

Believing in God does not necessarily mean accepting traditional religious views, such as the notions of personal immortality heaven, and hell. Personal immortality seems rather a rival to belief in God than a logical consequence of it. It is God who never dies, not humanity. Our sphere of action is on this planet, or eventually in this solar system and perhaps galaxy, between birth and death. As Robert Frost said, "Earth's the right place for love: I don't know where it's likely to go better."

Is it an intelligent view that the only value our lives will have after they are over is in the faint echoes and influences which may linger in human memory and human life? Can we really live merely for posterity, from a long-run point of view? I believe not. And if you say that we live partly for our own sakes, for the sheer joy of living, then I reply, "yes, indeed, but I am speaking of 'the long-run,'" and in the long run, we and our joys are, from the naturalistic point of view, not there at all. If you say, we live merely for the present moment, I reply, not even the higher animals can do that, and from a rational point of view, once the future is brought in, is it not arbitrary to stop at one's own death, or that of one's grandchildren?

As each of us lives on, from time to time some of our cells die. But what of it? We do not hesitate to suppose that the cells are there chiefly for our benefit, and if some of them die, do we not go on, and is not their contribution to our experience in some degree preserved in our memories? After all, the parts are for the sake of the whole. We readily see and accept this where we are the wholes, but is it not rational to say the same even where we are the parts and not the whole? Each of us is at least a part of humanity; but is that the ultimate whole of which we are parts? Is not humanity itself a fragment in space-time?

Only a cosmic life, it seems, can be the real whole for the sake of which all exists. We humans are such egoists that we try every trick, and every evasion to miss the point; yet I cannot but think that if our species survives long enough, we will at last weary of these evasions and accept the obvious principle that the inclusive reality must contain all the values, but then must not the inclusive reality be the proper object of worship, the real divinity? Some say, God is our highest ideal, but what about the cosmos? Does a fragment set the goal for the entirety of things? Our view of God may be our highest ideal, but must not God propose the ideal, the directive, for the cosmos?

The laws of nature are there to show that the ultimate directive does not come from human beings. Were we consulted in the setting of these laws? We guess the divine or cosmic ideal as best we can from observation, reasoning, and intuition. Traditional religions have treasured some of the results of past efforts in this direction.

We should neither ignore these treasures nor assume their correctness. Human fallibility has seen to it that they contain many a confusion, one-sidedness, or self-serving illusion. All worship has been haunted by the specter of idolatry. Each generation must wrestle anew with the mixture. Is it not a pity to worship less-than-God?

Charles Hartshorne

THEISTIC HUMANISM

The question is, do we live for ourselves and other human beings alone, or do we live for something in principle superior to humanity? The word "alone" is important. No one can help living for oneself and others, for no one is completely indifferent to his or her own fate and no one is wholly without fellow feeling. In the Judeo-Christian religion, and to a considerable extent in all religions, we are expected to love ourselves and are admonished to love their neighbor likewise. So far, humanism is an element in religion in general. One might think that theistic religion can only add; besides loving humanity love also God, but this will not do. God is so conceived that there can be no mere also. God is not just another object of devotion "Thou shalt love God with all thy heart and with all thy soul and with all thy mind and with thy strength." How could language say more plainly that God is the total object of loyalty. There is to be nothing in the person which is not love of God. How, then, can there be love of self and neighbor? Only in one way: if we are all entirely included in the divine reality. If pantheism meant only that there is nothing outside God, then in my opinion pantheism would be religiously imperative. Historically the term has had further meanings which I do not wish now to consider but which have given it unpleasant connotations. Theism does not add an additional object of devotion to those of humanism; it claims to make explicit the full context of the ordinary objects. It claims to reveal what human beings really are, namely members of the divine life. There are, for theism, no people outside God to love, but only people in God who would be bare nonentity except for this status in the divine.

This means that theism fully and without residue embraces humanism, except for the latter's negations. Any form of theism of

25

which this cannot be said is merely a perversion. It may be that many an orthodoxy is tainted with such perversion; I have here no concern with what is orthodox or heretical, apart form the orthodoxy that God is to be loved as total object of loyalty. In my opinion this is entirely capable of justification by secular philosophy, without appeal to revelation. There is no reasonable way to conceive God as merely another important reality besides the ordinary ones. Such a reality would be as ineffective in meeting the requirements of philosophical rationality as in fulfilling those of high religion. It would be one more item to explain, not the universal principle of explanation.

Theism is not an alternative to humanism as a positive system of values. It neither adds nor subtracts, except in a subjective sense. Subjectively it adds consciousness of what unconsciously, according to the claims of theism, must already have been there in experience. It makes the implicit explicit, that is all. It makes clear what the humanity we love not only is—but alone could possibly be—namely some portion of the content of the cosmic Life. Let us attempt to sketch some of the advantages of lifting this implication into consciousness, rather than leaving it to unanalyzed, unsymbolized feeling.

If humanity is a final end in itself, not constitutive of a superhuman life and value, what then? The most glaring difficulty is that of transience. Our experience is ever fleeting. That we die is hardly the essential aspect of this transience. Anyone's youth is already dead when he/she is middle-aged. Indeed, each yesterday is dead today. Yesterday I was in heaven; today I have discovered that this joy was based on an illusion; today I am in grief. What good now is that having been joyous a short time ago? A few faint echoes in present consciousness are all that is left of tens of thousands of past experiences, many of them vivid and rich when they were present. Compared to this wholesale loss of values, death, wars, pestilences are minor threats to the meaning of our lives if we think rationally about our existence. We talk of posterity, children, works of art and of science, and practical achievements as means of handing on value to the future, but all these are beside the main point. Nothing has value save experiences, and every experience is fleeting, a bubble about to burst. If, even for me, youth is already lost, save for a few evershifting echoes in the present, will it not be even more lost in posterity, which will not even have these echoes?

The problem of transience is that of unity of value through time. Each present has value, but only while it is present, it seems. Most of us strive not merely to be happy just now, but to be happy through as much of a long life as possible and this we desire for our children and friends as well. Where, however, in what present, is there such a thing a "happiness throughout a long life?" Actually there seems to be only happiness now, whatever the now may be. Thus value seems, from the human standpoint, to lack unity through time. We aim at total value: at the very least, happiness of lives, and this cannot be actual in human terms. Still less can the happiness of humanity, through the generations, ever be an actuality. Only happiness now seems real, but it is not happiness now that satisfies us as a goal. Indeed, happiness now is not a goal, but rather the satisfaction gained in pursuing the goal. Happiness is not presently aimed at, but the joy of aiming.

There is another problem, that of unity through space. One lives partly for self, partly for others, but how can our purpose be thus split up? What is the overall or total objective? We speak of the general welfare. But in what experience is the general welfare an actuality? Who really cashes in on the "happiness of humanity?" Surely no human being can do this. How can one add together one's happiness and that of every other person into a greatest happiness of humanity. Yet, unless we are selfish, must we not in principle live for some such inclusive happiness even though no such happiness seems to exist. There is only my happiness, your happiness but not a happiness consisting of mine and yours.

In both cases, the question of unity of value through time and of such unity through space, humanity apart from anything superhuman does not furnish what seems implicit in our purposes, but humanity does furnish the clue to the nature of the unity involved. The clue in the case of time is memory, in the case of space is sympathy. Both are perhaps only one basic function, since memory is a sort of sympathy with one's past experiences. There are, we have said, a few faint, ever changing echoes of past experiences in present experience. Experience is not absolutely evanescent. True, nearly all the vividness of the tens or hundreds of thousands of previous experiences is lost to us now, it being plainly impossible to crowd them into a human present except in the form of exceedingly dim or subconscious memories. Thus, there is no effective unity of value through time in simply human terms, but there is a principle operative which, in a radically superior mode of operation, would constitute an effective unity. If the attention span could expand just as fast as new experiences were actualized, so that memory need not be pale or subconscious but could be wholly vivid and distinct, then indeed having been happy through a long life would be an actual value in the present. The goal of striving would be achievable. Similarly, whereas our sympathy with our neighbors in space is slight, everfluctuating, there might be a sympathy not thus restricted, but effectively participant in the lives of all the denizens of space. A life whose present always preserved consciously all lives no matter how remote in the past and no matter where in space would be one whose value included and made actual the total general welfare we aim to promote as humanists. All the humanist values would be accepted, but it would no longer be an excruciating and unrelieved paradox how out of these values a general or total good could be formed by means of which the relative importance of various ends could in principle be measured.

In my opinion, a theism which understands itself (there has not been too much of such theism, I dare to think) will realize that "God" stands for something that, whatever other aspects it may have, conforms to the above stipulation. The divine life "inherits" all our experience, in its full vividness of individuality, and cherishes it forevermore. This is not well expressed by saying that we become mere means to the divine self-realization or fulfillment. For we enjoy our fleeting experiences as contributory to the divine experience, and it is good that such an experience was realized; or, here is a good experience and whatever may come it will be at least something that it has occurred, but for whom will it be something that has occurred. Not, save fleetingly, for ourselves. Not for posterity. What will they have of my experience? Besides, there might not always be a posterity? The only way to make conscious what is involved is to make conscious the implication that though we forget, not only others but even ourselves, our own precious experiences, there is that which never forgets and which always treasures our achievements of joy and beauty. A something which will be our definitive posterity and heir. To lose this something is only to love that which makes sense out of our aims. People have loved all sorts of fantastic things because they thought these things made sense out of their aims. How can we separate ourselves from our aims, or our aims from their implications? Only by self-misunderstanding can we fail to love God, if God is the aim of all our aims.

What practical value is there in all this? From one aspect, the answer has just been hinted at. If we do not see the reasonable aim implicit in all our aims, we set up an unreasonable one. We try to think of something less than deity as the inclusive and imperishable good. We pretend we will never die, we try to build indestructible tombs; we half forget humanistic values while we dream of a heaven "beyond the bounds of space and time;" we try to think of the state as the sole important heir of our achievement; we dream of human omnipotence and all-sympathetic goodness, while the modest powers and virtues really open to us are not cultivated. Everywhere we seek something perfect or quasiperfect, something lasting or quasi lasting, some inclusive or quasi inclusive good. Everywhere, too, we are disappointed and frustrated in this search (except as we find God). Still worse, the real human possibilities are overlooked. We long for the perfect and the abiding and the inclusive. This longing is either just stultified, repressed, and the whole zest for life weakened in apathy or cynicism; or it is expressed; and if expressed, then either through illusion, through some more or less dangerous idolatry, or through truly finding the One whose Life really abides and really inherits all our achievements, and really is perfect in its power of making a synthesis of these achievements, doing with them all that their value permits.

The divine perfection is not simply the inclusiveness of the divine sympathy in time and space, but the ideal way in which the "data" are woven together in a total experience than which no experience of those data could be more beautiful. True, this beauty cannot be our conscious possession, but those who die for a cause and do not themselves enter the promised land do not necessarily die discontented. That the land will be entered is the sense of our aim, not that we shall enter it. That the other who enters is not even human but radically superhuman— well, it is a strange doctrine that we can only love our equals. We can only have the love of equal companionship with equals, but there is another love, love of the one whose sympathy for us is infinitely more complete than even our self-sympathy. How shall one not love One whose love for us is the ideal which our self-love could never approach? God loves all our past, which we almost entirely fail vividly to recall, and all the dim depths of our present potentialities for the future, of which we are only slightly conscious. In love for the One who loves all, our love for all can be entirely included and unified. This humanism, past forms of theism have all too often failed to elucidate. Perhaps, after all, it is the future, more than the past, which must show what both humanists and theists have really been driving at.

THE MODERN WORLD
AND A MODERN VIEW OF GOD

Human self deification is a chief rival in our time of what I regard as true religion. For I agree with the old Greeks, who agreed with the Hebrews at this point, that one of our greatest enemies is our own vanity, hubris.

There are, however, several excuses for our modern falling deeply into hubris. Not only are our technology and pure science wonderful achievements, truly deserving to be glorified, but also these new powers encourage habits of thinking which in some respects make it more difficult to see grounds for belief in the superhuman. Science is our great theoretical accomplishment; yet it seems to uncover no evidence of anything divine. We have learned, or think we have learned, that what science cannot discover is very likely not there. If fairies and demons and witches were real, science would have had to invoke them to explain events. But it has no occasion to do so. Hence we cease to take such ideas seriously. The idea of God seems to many to belong in the same class, and we feel a certain obligation to be on the side of science, against fairy tales and nightmares.

Now I wish to argue that while all these reactions to the modern scene are natural enough, some of them do not withstand careful criticism and represent, indeed, aspects of a sort of fairy tale of science, not a tested scientific hypothesis.

So far as influencing nature is concerned, we have certainly immensely increased our resources. But the chief results of this change are: 1) the total number of people on earth has multiplied many times over, and has even become one of our gravest anxieties, a threat which only fatuous optimists belittle, 2) newborn babies have several times as

31

good a chance of reaching maturity as they used to have, 3) those who reach maturity can expect to live a decade or two longer than formerly, 4) A minority of people on earth have luxuries undreamed of in older days even for kings, and 5) when things go wrong, there is usually something we can do besides pray—we can look for an expert, medical or other, and we have better reason to trust our modern experts than the primitive had to trust elders and medicine men. However, do these differences amount to anything, relative to the problem of God? I say that, relative to that problem, they are negligible. Each of us is still born and dies; each is still throughout life subject to accidental death or grievous injury and are still but a negligibly small part of a stupendous whole, which for all we know infinitely precedes and will infinitely outlast us. Though armed with atomic power, humanity is yet almost nothing in physical power compared even to the sun, and there are billions and billions of suns! On this earth now, we are powerful, but what are we in the vastness of reality? So close to nothing we can scarcely say how small, or how weak.

In what I have just said, I have employed facts of astronomy. I think, indeed, that the proper result of science is to increase human humility, to make our inveterate conceit seem even more absurd, if possible, than the Greeks and ancient Hebrews could know it to be. Think of millions of galaxies, each probably with millions of planets. Even though we do reach a few of these planets in space ships, the ones we do not reach will be practically the same in number as all those which exist. Thus the races of rational beings which, according to all reasonable probability, people the great spaces, will be virtually unknown to us forever. The Greeks could explore but a small portion of this earth; they estimated the total universe as a billion miles in diameter. We talk in billions of light-years. True, we can explore our solar system, and eventually perhaps a bit beyond, but our solar system dwarfs the area of the earth which the Greeks could reach no more than our present estimate of the universe dwarfs that of the Greeks. Understating the case, no larger part of the universe, relatively speaking, seems to astronomers today open to human exploration than ancient astronomers supposed was open to it. Our relative insignificance, therefore, according to our knowledge, has not diminished. Only human vanity has enabled us to imagine otherwise—to talk, for example, of conquering space.

I am not, please note, belittling science. It is one of our noblest, most glorious accomplishments. But one of the chief origins of science— Einstein has said it—is deep humility. We are the only terrestrial animal, though surely not the only animal, who can see ourselves as but an item in the scheme of things, not the center about which all must or can be made to turn.

There is another consideration. Ancient people might dream of existing forever on earth. They did not know that the sun's fires are temporary and must eventually burn out. We do know. We also know that the sun might become unbearably hot, and destroy us in that way. We know that we have but a temporary dwelling on this earth. Of course, some of us may colonize other planets and even solar systems. But still, every such venture will be risky, many will fail; success can never be guaranteed, and certainly there is no guarantee that the successful colonists will be such as we would be able to consider in significant degree our own descendants, or even that our influence will have been helpful to them. Add to this the fact, which we know far better than ancient people, that human folly could bring human life to an end at almost any time—in the near or distant future.

We are not God and are infinitely far from being so. Rather we are a tiny, and for all practical purposes ultimately temporary, as well as unreliable and often very cruel, creatures. Now there are two possibilities and only two: this tiny, temporary episode of nature called humanity either exists merely for its own sake, or also for the sake of something greater than humanity. If we in our own eyes exist merely for ourselves, then so far as our valuations go, the rest of the universe exists for us. We must either serve, or be served by, the larger cosmos. We cannot but use the cosmos, so far as accessible to us, just as the cells in our bodies cannot but profit by our organic existence enclosing them, but the cells in our bodies also serve us whether or not they have any feeling of doing so. One way to put the religious question is simply: "Do we in turn stand in an analogous relation to anything greater than ourselves in space time, and can we have any awareness of this relation?"

This question has no proper analogy to that of fairies. Fairies at most were incidental conveniences, or nuisances. But the question, "Is the part for the whole, or the whole for the part?" is not an incidental question. It is the question, if we set aside our natural self-centeredness and look at life objectively, as the astronomer does. Are we to live and die merely for humanity, and are the species of rational animals on other planets to live and die merely for themselves? Or do they, and all creatures, live and die for the whole encompassing them, as our cells do for us?

Science as I view it could not possibly favor the self-centered answer to this question. Science is not anthropomorphic. It does not assume any peculiar importance of human beings. The famous "rejection of final clauses" was really, in one aspect, a rejection of human favoring causes. Nothing cosmic turns, for science, upon human values in particular. Does it follow that nothing turns upon values of any kind? I believe this is a non sequitur. The ends of nature could only be incomparably vaster than merely human ends and, therefore, we in our amazing vanity cannot easily conceive these ends. But they can be conceived, as we shall see.

Still, you may say, it remains true that science finds no evidence of anything divine, and where there is no scientific evidence, have we not learned to admit that there is no evidence at all? Here it is pertinent to inquire what it means to speak of scientific evidence. The highest, or at least, a very high authority on the scientific method, in my opinion is Karl Popper. His view is that a hypothesis is scientific if it can be observationally falsified, not, please note, if it can be verified. For it is doubtful if, strictly speaking, any scientific generalization has been verified, that is, shown to be exactly true as it stands. So-called crucial experiments are not those which have a chance of proving some theory since no experiment can wholly establish a positive theory; but rather, those which have a chance of disproving a theory. One instance clearly not in accordance with a supposed law refutes the law, but many instances in conformity with the law still do not prove it. Accepting this test of falsifiability, we may remark that the idea of God either could, or could not, be falsified by some conceivable observation. If it could not, then theism is a view which science is in no position to test; and the fact that science has not "verified" theism is irrelevant. For as, Popper persuasively argues, to confirm a view by scientific evidence is only to conceive a way of falsifying it, and then to find that the falsifying observation fails to result from the suitable experimental or observational conditions. Who, then, has told us what an observation incompatible with theism would be like? Is it the observation that there are evils? In that case, science is not needed to evaluate theism, for this fact has always been known. And theists have always denied that the existence of evils contradicted their belief. If they are right in this, then how could science find evidence against the divine existence? Is any fact, other than evil, incompatible with that existence? Is it the reign of law in nature? But theists say that the laws of nature express the divine power and consistency.

What are we to conclude from the apparent fact that theism, as theists understand it, is not scientifically testable at all? We might conclude that theism has no consistent meaning, and hence could not be true. Or we might conclude that it has some meaning, but of a sort whose truth is untestable by human means. Finally, we might conclude that it has meaning, and that science is not the only human means of testing truth. This last is my position. I hold that the relevant test of ideas of God is their ability to integrate, not facts of science, but the principles which all science and all life presuppose, principles without which we could not understand how there could be facts at all, or why it is worth knowing what the facts are. Not facts, but the ideas of fact, not values but the idea of value, not truths but the idea of truth, is what theism tries to elucidate. The study which investigates such questions is philosophy. To suppose that natural science can substitute for philosophy in this task is logical confusion; it is pseudo science, not science.

Are theists right, however, in holding that the facts of evil and of the orderliness of nature are consistent with theism? I hold that they are right. However, I do not think that the classical, or best known, theologians and theistic philosophers have given us a very clear and consistent account of this matter, and I cannot blame anyone who concludes that they have failed to make their case. I shall now try to show how the case can be made.

It is useless to maintain that all evil is divinely designed and is but good in disguise, for on that principle all human choice is absurd. Do as you please, the result is exactly what divine wisdom saw to be needed for the perfection of the world plan. True, it may be a part of the plan that you should be punished for what you do, but still your deed is quite as it should be, for if it were not, it would not have been included in the providential design, and would not have happened. On this view, serving God means doing whatever you happen to do. You cannot go wrong. In addition to this absurdity, is the difficulty of distinguishing between such a God and the sadist who finds evil to his or her liking. God deliberately designs the evils, for they are necessary to the world's being pleasing to God.

It is also useless to explain evil as the result of human freedom alone, for all animate nature involves conflict and presumably suffering. Surely human choice throws no light upon this fact.

The root of the trouble is in failing to note the starting point for the problem of evil. This starting point is the notion that God creates. What is it to create? It is to determine the otherwise indeterminate. Out of the vagueness or chaos of the merely possible, comes the definiteness of the actual. There might be all sorts of worlds: yet this world came into being. Similarly, the poet might write all sorts of poems, but actually writes this poem, or this set of poems. Now suppose the divine poet includes in a poem a description of a lesser non-divine or human poet creating non-divine poetry. The divine poet can choose the description of this other and lesser poet and poetry just as is pleasing, can God not? No, this will not do, for the divine poet creates not just poems, but poets who create poems; and since to create is to decide how the vagueness of possibility is to pass into definite actuality, if the created poets really exist as poets, as creators, then they, and not the divine poet must decide in some degree what the non-divine poems are to be. I wonder if you see already how, according to this analysis, the problem of evil results from an equivocation of terms. According to the view which gives rise to the problem, God is to decide precisely what lesser agents decide; but then there can be no lesser agents, and all decisions are divine decisions. The supreme artist would thus create not lesser artists, but mere descriptions of artists, mere dreams of lesser creators. The one agent is, on that view, the only agent, but imagines others. We are these divine imaginings of lesser agents. But in that case, we could from our own experience have no concept of creation, of agency, of decision, with which to ascribe the supreme form of these powers to deity. The whole business is a play with ambiguities, and I believe it is nothing more.

Once you admit that the supreme artist must create lesser artists, with genuine, though inferior capacities for deciding what no one else has wholly decided for them, you will see that the perfection of divine power cannot consist of a monopoly of creative freedom. However well and powerfully God may decide, God must leave something for the creatures to decide. Hence it cannot be right to attribute the details of the world to divine decree, and it need not be wrong to attribute the evils of these details to decisions other than divine. Nor is it merely human creatures who must in some measure have creative power, for what could the supreme creative agent produce but lesser forms of creativity? There is no absolute difference between human originality and that of an humble animal tracing the design of its own individual life in fine details unique and never to be repeated. The jump from infinite creativity to the creature, even the humble creature, can hardly be from the infinite to zero; it must rather be from the infinite to the finite, from supreme creative freedom to lesser creative freedom, not no freedom. Any creature is thus somewhere between the total absence of discretionary power, and its eminent or divine form. In this way creaturely freedom explains not only evils which man produces but those which animals and atoms produce. The entire world, on a consistently theistic view, is pervaded by an element of self-determination in each and every individual whatsoever. Myriads of agents other than God have had a hand in any result, and it is therefore illegitimate to ask why God made that result as it is. God did not "make" it, if that means decide it, for the creatures are all, in part, self-decided.

Does it follow that we must renounce the perfection of the divine power? Not if words are used carefully. The perfection of the divine power does not consist of the ability to make merely unilateral decisions, for this is meaningless. Every agent and every creator produces results beyond itself only by influencing the self-determination of other agents, or other creators. Decision is always shared, so far as effects upon others are concerned. The perfect form of this shared decision means, not ideal ability to decide detailed results, but ideal ability to decide general outlines. These outlines are the laws of nature. Who but God could have decided these? They set the limits within which the lesser agents can effectively work out the details of their existence. Without such limits the universal creativity would mean universal chaos and frustration. With these limits, elements of chaos and frustration remain but they are subordinate to general order and harmony.

The orderliness of nature is essential to creaturely freedom. It can then, without inconsistency, be considered providential. That some evils result is not the fault of the order, for any order must stop short of destroying freedom, and freedom means risk.

To put the matter another way, the atheistic argument from evil holds that God must be weak or wicked in not using divine freedom to maximize harmony and reduce discord to zero. This means nothing if not this, that the chances of harmony and those of discord could and should be made to vary inversely., but we can, rather clearly, understand that this is logically impossible. Harmony and discord, as values, have the very same source, freedom. Harmony in freedom is good, conflict in freedom is evil, and the greater the freedom the greater the chances of both good and of evil. God is held deficient for not doing what logically could not be done. To avoid the evil of suffering and discord, God should have a world of pure puppets, incapable of getting off their designated tracks; to avoid the evil of deadly monotony and insipidity, to make existence interesting by causing free agents able to make their own decisions to flourish, he should not have a world of puppets at all, but self-determining creatures with some faint spark at least of creativity analogous to his own supreme creativity.

I see nothing in the classic "problem of evil" but this confusion or equivocation between creatures both puppets and free, or both lesser forms and not even lesser forms of the power of decision eminently ascribed to their creator.

The ideal power and wisdom of God does not, then, imply a perfection of detailed results, for no power could guarantee the detailed actions of others but rather an optimal excess of opportunity over risk, as arising from the laws of nature.

I cannot give anything like all my reasons for accepting this conception, but I wish to return to our previous question: "Is the part for the sake of whole, or the whole merely for the sake of the part?" To me it seems wonderfully irrational to suppose that the enduring universe exists merely for its transient parts, but if the parts exist for the whole, then the whole must contain the values of the parts. Since it is unintelligible that values can exist except for some being able to value or enjoy them, the cosmos should be thought of as able to value all that falls within it. The supreme creator is then the whole, evolving and appreciating its own parts, somewhat as the human body evolves new molecules, and in many cases new cells, from time to time; but the supreme whole must have full appreciation, such as we cannot have, for the details of the parts. The idea of the cosmos as conscious and evolving its own details, subject to their proper freedom is, I believe, compatible with all the results of science. True, there are many puzzles which may arise in this connection, but it is striking how few among the skeptics see that this is the question to which theists, if they understand themselves, give an affirmative answer. Most theists are unclear about this also, and many will say that I am quite on the wrong track, but I believe I have read these people with more care than they have read me, or anyone who thinks as I do.

I said above that science excludes not all final causes, but human favoring or anthropocentric final causes. I shall now try to explain this. One must first understand, once and for all, that no teleology can exclude unfortunate accidents and frustrations, for goals have to be reached through multiple acts of freedom, none of which can be entirely controlled, even by God. The point is not that God cannot control them, but that they cannot be controlled. It is not God's influence which has limits, but their capacity to receive influence. Absolute control of a free being, and there can be no others, is self-contradictory. Hence exceptional monstrosities and incidental sufferings are to be attributed to the chance results of freedom, not to the teleology of nature. Only the general plan, the structure of laws, the normal pattern of nature can be wholly purposive.

If you ask, must not the laws and the antecedent conditions entirely determine the detailed phenomena, the answer is, not if law is conceived as physicists now incline to conceive it, as essentially statistical, a matter of averages in a large group of similar cases. The new outlook in physics thus fits our doctrine of pervasive freedom, as the Newtonian outlook did not.

Granting then that details are not necessarily purposive, what are the goals which nature is realizing? Here older discussions, both theistic and antitheistic, suffered from arbitrary assumption. For instance, it was thought strange that all living creatures are subject to death, that species die out, that creatures live by destroying other creatures. I find all of these things less strange than the more or less unconscious beliefs which made them appear strange. Is it desirable for an individual to live forever? If the individual has no long run memory and foresight, it cannot matter to it that it will not live forever, and if the individual does not have long range memory and foresight, then in the long run continuation within the limits of its individuality will prove increasingly monotonous, lacking in interest and zest. All young animals show more evidence of being thrilled by life, the novelty of things, than old animals. Human beings are not exceptions, in principle. They only think they are. One has but to observe life to see this. So I conclude, endless continuation of the individual is either of no value to the individual, or it is undesirable, even unendurable. That species do not last forever is even more obviously not an evil. Species other than us cannot know that they are temporary, and we can understand how our temporary existence can contribute to what is not temporary, the all-encompassing Whole.

You may suppose that even the Whole, according to the same principle of diminishing novelty, must finally grow old and tired, but the whole is the supreme reality, with no external conditions limiting it; whatever novelty it may need, it should have full power to evolve. Only ideal power, divine power, can either sustain, or make desirable, endless continuation. So I think we can, quite consistently, conceive God as immortal, without giving up the argument that mortality for creatures is an evil for them. Something in reality must be permanent, and God, I submit, is precisely that something.

But should creatures live, while they do live, by destroying others? Is this not vicious or cruel? This too I deny. Granted that creatures should not live forever, how then are they to die? The only causes must be other creatures, either within, as parts, or without as members of the external environment. What harm does it do a deer that it dies through the attack of a lion, rather than of old age? Old age is a dull mode of existence; if death generally came that way, then instead of the species being composed mostly of creatures enjoying the prime of Life, it would be more largely composed of half bored elders. The sum of intense enjoyment would be less, not more.

What, we now ask, are the overall goals of nature? We have argued that the parts live not merely for their own sakes but for that of the whole. What does the whole get from the parts? Well, what do we get from our parts, our bodily cells and molecules? We get the sensory and emotional content of our experience. When our cells thrive, we feel physical pleasure; when they are injured, we often feel physical pain. Thus their health contributes to our joy, and their ill health to our sorrow. We seem to participate in their weal and woe in whatever sense they are subject to weal and woe. Cells are living—I believe sentient—individuals. The "love of God" has often been spoken of, but we may overlook the full meaning of our own words. To love is, at least, to participate in the life of another. It may be more than that, but we should not use the word for less. We love, then, our own cells, though without distinct consciousness, so far as the single cells are concerned. We have a vague sense of good and evil enjoyed by the parts of the body. Imagine this vague sense flooded with the light of full consciousness and you have an analogy for the love of God.

It is a well known law that the value of experience as coming to us from the body depends upon the variety and intensity of activities which can be harmonized. We know that lack of variety and contrast kills interest; we also know that variety and contrast may in some cases confuse and disturb. Harmonious variety is essential to value. What is nature if not a wondrously varied pattern of forms. Is it an harmonious pattern? Not in the sense of excluding all conflict, discord, or suffering; but this we have seen to be inherent in the pervasiveness of freedom, without which there could be no world at all. Essentially nature is harmonious, things fit together in an ecological web which naturalists admire the more they study it. The laws of nature articulate the harmony of nature. Some of the greatest scientists have tried to tell us how their more or less mystical reverence for and enjoyment of the cosmic harmony inspires their work, but we have often been too dull to believe them. I take them at their word.

Nature is a harmony in variety, ultimately for the enjoyment of the whole, but proximately for the enjoyment of each and every part, in proportion to its awareness of this harmony. Variety is in space as well as in time. That individuals and species die and others take their place is variety in time. Those who lament the passing of species want to limit the variety to be enjoyed by the whole. Truly they know not what they would have.

41

Can God love us if we are allowed to cease while God lives on? The answer lies in a simple ambiguity in the word "cease." That our lives are finite in time as well as in space does not mean that at death we become nothing, or a mere corpse, for our past experiences are not canceled out. The past is indestructible, ever-living. Persons who truly love those who have died feel this vividly, though they usually, thanks to the strange blinders worn by philosopher and theologians who have taught them no better, misconceive the nature of the feeling. The past reality of the person is not dead and cannot die. It "lives forevermore," in Whitehead's phrase. Where? How? In the Whole, whose appreciation is infinitely tenacious of every item it once has appropriated. God forgets us never, and this is our immortality. We are imperishable items in God's consciousness.

Our vanity is perhaps not satisfied by this. I can only speak for myself. I wish no further immortality, either for myself or for those I love. It is this earthly life which should be dear to us, for which we should be grateful, and this life is deathless, for what we and those we have influenced have done and felt cannot ever not have been done and felt, but the ultimate summing up and treasuring of this imperishable reality is not in our memory of consciousness; it is in God's.

There will be those who say that the view I have been presenting is pantheistic, implying that this is enough to condemn it. The term "pantheism" has been used to cover doctrines as far apart from each other as from views commonly called theistic, and the habit of trying to put an end to reasonable discussion by the use of this label is on a par intellectually with terming every economic policy with which we disagree "communist." The communism which properly deserves rejection in principle is something much more definite that those who misuse the term have in mind; so with the pantheism which deserves rejection in principle. Or, in other words, if my view is pantheistic, then perhaps so much the better for (one form of) pantheism, not necessarily so much the worse for my view.

The foregoing conception of God, or something like it, can be found, apart from my own writings, in Fechner's Zend Avesta, written a century ago, in Berdyaev's The Destiny of Man, and in the last chapter of Whitehead's Process and Reality. Many other writers have pointed in its direction. It is the great neglected alternative to classical theism, the stone rejected by the builders, whose ultimate destiny has by no means been decided by this rejection.

But how, you may ask, can we know any such view to be true? The answer to this question is a long story, but it can summarized in brief as follows: that philosophy is true which contains in itself the explanatory power of its rival, plus additional power of its own. The theory of pervasive freedom explains evil at least as well as any other view could do, for freedom is always risk, but the theory explains good better than other view, provided we admit a supreme or divine level of freedom, by whose influence all lesser freedom can be benignly guided and coordinated, for freedom thus coordinated is primarily opportunity, and only secondarily risk. Thus freedom, if taken as both divine and non-divine is self-explanatory, accounting alike for its failures and its successes. It is the only self-explanatory principle. Order is due to the overruling supremacy of divine freedom, disorder to the multiplicity of lesser freedoms.

An interesting, but complicated, matter to reconsider is the historical proofs for the existence of God in the light of this modern doctrine. I find that in spite of the attacks of Hume, Kant, and others, they can all be restated so as to have a certain cogency.

These attacks rest upon assumptions incompatible with the theory of pervasive freedom, and of divine freedom as that of the all-inclusive reality. If we are not to be victimized by mistakes of our ancestors, the entire problem of God must be viewed afresh. I deeply believe that the idea of a God who determines all things is an absurdity; and I also deeply believe that religion without God is a poor second best, an irrational self deification of humanity in our dangerous pride. Our life is on earth, not elsewhere; but the eventual importance of earthly life consists of its contribution to the cosmic Life, which alone is truly immortal, and alone deserves to be worshipped.

Charles Hartshorne

A NEW WORLD AND NEW WORLD VIEW

In the last hundred years a philosophical and theological change has occurred, but it is one you will not read about in the newspapers or even in most textbooks and histories of philosophy. Nature includes two extremes: one is the inanimate aspect, studied in physics, astronomy, and similar sciences; the other, the human aspect, is studied in psychology, history, and the humanities. Between these extremes are many degrees of the animate in plants and the subhuman animal species. For philosophy, the question has been which extreme exhibits more clearly the general principles of nature. The first option is to take inanimate nature, so far is it is known to common sense or to science before quantum physics, as the model of reality in general and assimilate the animate and even the human to this model. Materialism and mechanism represent this option. Even human freedom is viewed as a special, complicated case of deterministic causality. People are analyzed as complex machines. A second option is to view the inanimate world as in the first case—that is, purely materialistically and mechanistically— but to make an exception at least of human species and perhaps of all animals, admitting that they are not mere machines but more or less conscious organisms, which at least in the higher forms, partially transcend strict causal determinism in their behavior. This second, or dualistic, option is really a cop-out, since it gives up the search for general principles of nature.

There is a third option, the last to be adequately worked out. It takes the human end of the scale of natural things as the model, since it is the one we know best, and views the degrees of animation from single cells to increasingly complex forms of multicellular animals as

45

stages in the development from low to high degrees of awareness and freedom. To complete this view, one must see not single cells or viruses as the lowest level of awareness and freedom but the very molecules, atoms, and particles of so-called inanimate nature. In quantum theory, these entities appear as lively and organized creatures. The seeming lack of animation and organization in earth, air, liquids, and metals is, as Leibniz guessed long ago, an illusion of our senses. Furthermore, the strict determinism of classical physics is now seriously challenged or rejected by many, perhaps most, physicists. For all we can know, when an atom of uranium turns into an atom of lead, it may be a spontaneous act of the atom. No law determines when it happens.

The way is now open to try to understand molecules as simpler versions of what a cell is, and the cell as a vastly simpler version of what even a human animal is. As for plants, those large enough to be visible are, for botanists, colonies of cells. In this respect they are like animal embryos before the formation of a functioning nervous system. They are also somewhat like you or me when we are in dreamless sleep. Thus, all of nature is covered by our third option. Any insentient thing such as a cloud, a rock or river, or even a tree, is a crowd or swarm of invisibly small constituents that are very unlike what we know as rocks, rivers, clouds or trees; rather, on a vastly more primitive level, they resemble us in having their own self-activity. This activity is the external sign of mind and freedom, however humble or trifling in degree or quality.

There remains the question of God. As atoms are akin to us but unimaginably simpler and inferior, so God is like us but unimaginably superior and more complex. The crucial theological problem is whether we can reconcile the likeness and the difference. The God that Nietzsche declared dead had never really been alive because the reconciliation of these two requirements—likeness to life as we know it and superiority to all other living forms, actual or possible—had not been achieved. For nearly two millennia, God was thought of as an unmoved mover, wholly self-sufficient and uninfluenced by the world. Somehow this being was supposed by most theologians to act freely, rather than in a causally determined way. Causal laws were themselves taken to be free acts of God. In addition, God was supposed to love the creatures. Many theologians denied that human beings, at least since the Fall, had even the least spark of the freedom of action attributed to God, yet humanity was also said to be an image of God. Even those who allowed some human freedom did not allow our actions to have any influence on God.

This theology seems to many of us now to be riddled with absurdities. It made the problem of evil desperate indeed since it either deprived us of any creative power or it made us, along with God, exceptions to otherwise supposedly valid principles of intelligibility.

The alternative, now more clearly formulated than ever before, is to view mind and freedom as matters of degree, supreme in God, very slight in particles and atoms, gradually increasing through molecules and cells to the higher animals and ourselves. Contemporary physics fits this view far better than did the physics known to Leibniz, the grandfather of this third option.

The kind of philosophy I am talking about is shared, with secondary differences, by the Frenchman Henri Bergson, by the American Charles Peirce, by the Anglo-American Alfred North Whitehead, and in varying degrees, by others. In principle, it preceded quantum physics. Some call it "process philosophy." It changes everything. For example, it gives a new answer to the old question, "Why does God not prevent suffering and evil?" and also to the question, "Why do animals all die?" It gives a new meaning to the old formula that the proper aim of rational beings is to serve God. This statement used to mean one should obey a being for whom one could do nothing since the being is wholly self-sufficient and immutable. Now it can mean that one should make one's life as valuable a contribution as one can to the supreme or divine life, in somewhat the same way as the health of one's bodily cells contributes to one's well-being.

What follows is an item of Unitarian history that will be unfamiliar to many readers. Nearly four centuries ago, the Italian theologian Faustus Socinus criticized the traditional deification of Jesus of Nazareth; in addition, though scarcely any encyclopedia or history will say so, he rejected the traditional idea of God as an unmoved mover, an immutable and all-determining power. Believing that human beings have genuine freedom, Socinus denied that God either determines or eternally knows our free acts. Rather, we determine the acts, and God knows them only after the fact or as they occur.

This view implies real novelty in the divine consciousness, it means that we cause changes in God. In this bold break with tradition, Socinus anticipated our current process theology. What he chiefly lacked was the insight that the idea of creaturely freedom, which creates novelty even in God, should be generalized to apply to all creatures, even the humblest—for instance, atoms. Human creativity is then no sheer exception in an otherwise divinely determined world but is only an extremely special, high-level case of creaturely freedom. Before the physics of the late nineteenth century, this generalization could scarcely be entertained, but about a hundred years ago a number of thinkers, more or less independently, did entertain and defend it. Among them were Peirce, Boutroux and later Bergson, both in France, Varisco in Italy, and Whitehead.

Another important passage of theological history has been neglected. The father of American theology, Jonathan Edwards, was, as is well known, a theological determinist who believed divine power decides all our actions. What is less well known that the Unitarian-bred Ralph Waldo Emerson held the same belief, as his diary makes clear. I deeply admire Emerson, but in his religious metaphysics he was surprisingly close to Edwards. This is one of many instances of the sad fact that the metaphysical originality and courage of Socinus and his followers were for several centuries allowed to go for nothing. Another instance of their lying fallow is that when, some years ago, the Unitarian church of England drew up a statement of faith, God was defined as immutable in the document. Why labor the point? Three centuries were wasted by the failure of scholars to do their job in dealing the Socinianism. I had to read a little-known German work by Otto Fock entitled, Der Socinianismus, to find out what the Socinians believed about God.

I appreciate the difficulties many have with theism. As a college sophomore, I roomed with an atheistic senior, and I have associated much with nontheists ever since. Concerning difficulties with the idea of God, I ask, "Which idea? Is it the classical notion of an immutable being that decides the details of cosmic history in eternity?" Then I am an atheist. "Or is it the conception of God as supreme freedom and love responding to creatures, the least of which has some freedom of its own and at least some primitive form of what in a generalized sense could be called love—at a minimum, some spark of sympathy for others, some feeling of their feelings?" Whatever the difficulties presented by this idea, they are not the same as the problems with the more usual conception. Only this usual conception figures in the works of the great nontheistic writers from Carneades in ancient Greece to Feuerbach, Marx, Nietzsche, Russell, Dewey, Santayana, and Freud.

The phrase "free religion" ought, it seems, to mean more than mere independence from traditional or current thought; it should yield opportunity to choose the best in traditional or contemporary wisdom. To what extent is this being done?

Long ago certain truths were seen, but so were certain half-truths with which they are easily confused or which obscure their meaning. One truth seen long ago is that the only self-justifying ideal is to love others as we love ourselves. The major religions have taught this; it may be called the ultimate ideal, but other and partly incompatible ideals and beliefs have continually clouded that vision. Western philosophers, for the most part, have taught that we love ourselves because we are ourselves and love others only for our own sake. Enlightened self-interest was made the first principle, and altruism was taken as wholly derivative. This is not to love others as we love ourselves. What the ultimate ideal means is that one should love people, ourselves included, as one person among many. One should love oneself for the sake of others as truly as others for our own sakes. But few Western philosophers really understood this principle. Two who did were Peirce and Whitehead.

How can it be logical, you may ask, to love others not primarily for our own sakes but for their own? In Asia, the Buddhists saw the reason with a clarity denied to Aristotle, Augustine, Thomas Aquinas, and Immanuel Kant. David Hume perhaps came closest to seeing it before Peirce. The point is that self-identity—I with myself, you with yourselves throughout life—is a highly relative and partial identity. I am not simply and absolutely one with myself as a child and old man, asleep and awake, delirious or in my right mind. I am not simply different from other people. The truth is much subtler and more complex. Personal identity is not the key to love. Love is not something caring for itself; it is a relationship between two entities. If I love myself, then I and myself are genuinely two, not one. Thus, I, as I am right now, may love myself as I was yesterday or as I may be tomorrow. I may also feel antipathy toward my other selves. Nor is self-interest in the form of genuine care for one's own future automatic. Immediate pleasure often blots out any regard for future consequences, even to oneself.

Why should one aim at future good for anyone, even for oneself? In the long-term future, we are dead. Is it for the good of corpses that we are striving? Taking the whole future into account, the self is a wasting asset. To make it the ultimate good is to turn life into Macbeth's "tale/ Told by an idiot/full of sound and fury/Signifying nothing." An elder citizen like myself sees this fact more readily than the young are likely to; yet I was twenty years old when I first saw it.

Present experience, as I then began to understand, is a contribution, a gift, to future experience; otherwise, in ultimate perspective, it is indistinguishable from nothing. The present becomes the past for an ever new present, and in this perpetually renewed contribution to the future is our only permanent reality. To make a huge fuss about whether the new present that later inherits from this one will always be a state of self—rather than of descendants, pupils, friends, strangers, or even life in nonhuman for— is to show a failure to understand our mortal existence. The final question is what we can contribute to the future of life, any life that can be supposed able to receive and adequately appropriate our contribution.

Of course, we are all more or less selfish. Any vertebrate animal sees and feels itself as the center of the world, "Here I am; there you are, background for my career." As Reinhold Niebuhr saw so well, this feeling translates itself readily in a thinking animal into an egocentric attitude that carried to the limit, amounts to self-deification. Only a divine ego could be the real center of the world. Thus, our animal experience puts us at the center of the world, while our reason tells us that every other human person is as central as we are, so that neither is central. The other is, in principle, as permanent or impermanent as we are. As Shakespeare said, "We are such stuff/As dreams are made on, and our little life/Is rounded with a sleep." Unfortunately, much Western philosophy and, to some extent, nearly all philosophy and still more nearly all religion have cheated us here. They have flattered our individual or collective conceit with theories of personal immortality and have tried in every way to explain away death, instead of helping us to accept it for what it is. The ancient Jews were the great exception, honor to them. Even when individual death has been accepted, however, the human species has often been regarded as though it were immortal. Species do last longer than individuals, but they, too, are mortal, and basically for the same reason, that they are contingent creatures of the creative process, dependent for continued existence upon circumstances.

A newspaper report credits a professor of sociology with the memorable sentence, "Life promises us nothing but experience." In other words, all actual value is felt, enjoyed value. The rest is only the possibility of value, checks that can be cashed only in experience. Each experience is momentary; it falls into the past, where its only worth is in its value for new experience. What are my or your childhood experiences unless someone now remembers or benefits from them? At the time, we felt they were important, and so they were, but importance cannot be defined as a relation of the present to the present; it must be a relation to the future.

I call this doctrine "contributionism." Life now contributes to life in the future; only in this way can it have meaning or importance. Consider from this point of view our environmental problems. In principle, the energy crisis is centuries old. Nonrenewable resources are nonrenewable. Is poverty of resources to be our gift to posterity? Is it not time we faced the basic environmental truth that the destruction of nonrenewable resources depends largely on two factors, the size of the population and, above all, the average amount of luxurious and wasteful practices per person? Without care and a substantial measure of economic asceticism and of modesty in our material demands (even with a stable population, which we do not have), we shall make a sadly negative contribution to the material situation of posterity.

Our notorious waste of food comes partly from our fortunate share in the world's good agricultural land and our agricultural know-how, but there are other reasons. In pioneer times, physical exertion made more calories necessary than now, when so many of us do so little physically. In addition, although in this country we boast of our freedom, we have an odd tendency to expect individuals to differ little from one another. We do admit that smaller people need smaller suits of clothes, for instance, but furniture is made to fit a single standard sized person. Worst of all, meals are served largely in single standard sizes. You can buy a small or large glass of juice, but nearly everything else is served in a single amount that is the same for all and much beyond the needs of most people. Sometimes children's plates are serve—to children; but age is not the point. Adults as well as children vary widely in both size and physical habits, hence in their need for food. As a result of the way food is now served, one eats too much. Obesity has become a national disease. One wastes food, or one has the courage to ask for a doggie bag. The government has asked restaurants to serve food in small as well as large portions; so far there seems to have been no response. Until this irrational way of serving food is changed, the overeating, waste, and inconvenience will go on.

Emerson was a hero of my youth. Some years ago I found a new reason to admire him. When a group of women drew up a list of rights that society owed to women, Emerson wrote in his diary, "Of course they should have these things. It is very cheap to laugh at them." John Stuart Mill responded to the issue with his famous essay, The Subjection of Women. What did other men do at that time? Only when applied science had cut the death rate and lengthened life sufficiently to free women from having to spend most of their lives bearing and rearing children could the point be generally grasped, and there is still a long way to go.

Life is a gift from past life to future life. This simple truth goes deeper than we normally realize. The great singer Paul Robeson sang a moving song about four rivers all finding their way to the sea. To the question of questions, "Into what sea does all life pour its treasures?" I have found no nontheistic answer. Emerson's Oversoul or Plato's world soul is the only answer I know; but this soul, this divine life, is not to be conceived as immutable, for then our lives could not contribute to it, or as all-determining, for then all suffering and wickedness is its doing and our sense of freedom an illusion.

It is sometimes said that we are less ethical than our ancestors. Perhaps we are, but perhaps also, because of altered circumstances, what are called the same actions are not really the same because of changes in their effects. Whatever else is right, it is right to see things as they are. Our duty to love our neighbors is a duty to promote their welfare in actual situations, and technology keeps changing them. We should take these changes into account in considering our obligations. Augustine said, "Love God, and do as you please." In other words, accept the deep truth of reality as expressive of divine love, and you will want to act in a manner appropriate to that truth.

Let us not imagine that God is only the God of biblical times, ignorant of whatever the writers of the Old or New Testaments did not know that scientists, philosophers, or theologians are now aware of. Give God credit for knowing what is true, including truths only now being discovered by human beings. Some of these truths did not obtain in biblical times, even for God, since they have resulted from human decisions then not yet made, not yet there to be known. The changes in hygiene and medicine that have altered the position of women are important examples of new truths with ethical bearings. It is time people caught up with Emerson and Mill, those pioneers in ethical thinking about human relations. They were right in principle, but the technological resources were not yet available to make application of the ideal altogether feasible. Women should not have to submit to restrictions that made some sense a hundred or two thousand years ago. This principle is what the feminist movement is all about.

Here is another example. People who became senile used, for the most part, to die fairly soon. Now human vegetables are being kept alive for years. The resources used for this unworthy purpose could be better applied. Society needs to regard as a valid contract a document, like those many have already signed, asking to be allowed to die when life on a human plane is no longer possible. A human near vegetable is not a neighbor in the ethical sense. To allow such a creature, who is no longer human, to cease to exist can be called murder only by a gross misuse of that word. Are we to treat all destruction of animal life as murder? In that case, only vegetarians escape being murderers.

Is abortion murder? It may be objectionable, certainly sad, but to call it murder merely begs the ethical question. A fetus is not actually a humanly thinking creature but only one that may become so if at least one adult makes sufficient sacrifices to bring this development about. Is it the proper business of judges or legislators to decide whether these sacrifices shall be made? A fetus is in no reasonable sense of the word a person, a citizen, or neighbor. Also, given the doctrine of the separation of church and state, we cannot expect our laws to enforce principles that have no clear relation to known facts about which we might reach a consensus.

Unwanted pregnancy is a dismal business, and both men and women have a clear duty to try to avoid it. Our society fails badly here. Of course, a case can be made for bearing a child for which one feels unable to be a good parent and giving it to foster parents, but to demand that a person who does not want to bear a child should do so on the ground that the alternative is murder is verbal cheating. We hear talk of the "rights of the unborn." If a creature as mindless as an embryo a few weeks old has rights, why not horses? It is society, or pregnant women, or their lovers that have rights here, not embryos. Threatened with a population deficiency, a society might have a right to try to prevent abortion, but this would be not the embryo's right but society's, and it is doubtful if there is such a society anywhere today.

All animals have rights in the sense that it is immoral to treat them cruelly, but they do not have a right to live forever. When they shall die is a question over which the human species cannot entirely avoid exercising choice.

I have not discussed sexual ethics. This topic, if I were wise enough for it, would take up all my time. I will, however, tell you one thing that I know and hope you do, too: fidelity to one sexual partner through a lifetime can, with luck and good management, mean great happiness.

Charles Hartshorne

AMERICA FROM COLONIAL BEGINNINGS TO PHILOSOPHICAL GREATNESS

When the American colonists crossed, first the Atlantic, and then the mountains and the prairies on their way westward, they tended to leave certain things behind, the fine arts most obviously, but also theoretical science. Three things, however, were not left behind, at least not for long: the art of government, religion, and *philosophy*. The first could not be dispensed with, nor the second; and indeed, the very reasons for leaving the Old World were often intensely religious. Also philosophizing, like religion, is almost native to human beings as such. Moreover, the diversity of religions favored philosophical reflection, and it led to the early establishment of freedom of thought to a degree which had been uncommon in western civilization generally. So we need not be surprised that Jonathan Edwards was far better as a theologian and philosopher than any of the colonists was as a scientist. Down to the end of the nineteenth century the country produced only one natural scientist of superb quality, Willard Gibbs, and it is typical of the situation that few U. S. citizens have ever heard of him. Pure scientific theory was not greatly encouraged in a land where the need was for applications of existing knowledge to transform a wilderness into farms, habitations, roads, railroads, and other means of communication. The inventor, not the scientist, was most honored. Practicality was in order, but the political and religious questions were not to be evaded, and reflection upon them could be accepted as practical enough. Such reflections easily led into the depths of philosophy. Thus, it was perhaps almost predictable that Gibbs should have been followed by a half dozen philosophers great distinction and many others of only lesser merit. Europe does not yet quite realize it, but this was one of the supreme philosophical flowerings of all times and all lands.

It is supposed by many Europeans that most philosophical ideas originated in Europe and then, in a delayed and usually inferior form found their way across the Atlantic. Of course this has happened, but it has also happened that the first formulation appeared in this country, and in some cases Europe still has not caught up. Even when a European did say it first, the American version may have been independent—or, sometimes, an improvement not a diminution. Thus, Royce's version of the basic idealistic argument from epistemological to metaphysical idealism has elements which in clarity and cogency surpass anything in Berkeley or Hegel. Finally, in the Six Classical American Philosophers, so designated by Max Fisch, we have had a group not surpassed in any country during the past one hundred years. I doubt if it would be too much to say, not surpassed in all continental Europe. That Europe has not been aware of this is one of the not unnatural consequences of the situation. The provincialism of European countries, due in part to the two great wars and to other causes, is one reason they have not maintained the superiority with which they are accustomed to credit themselves.

I have been speaking of superiority in philosophy. Science is another matter. Here provincialism tends everywhere to be transcended, and besides, conditions in this country have been much less favorable for scientific than for philosophical creativity. What in Europe went into basic scientific reflection tended here (until recently at least) to go into secondary experimentation and applications. On the other hand, what in Europe went into the cultivation of each country's own philosophical heritage, or of its borrowings from Germany, here went into a courageous and informed confronting of the international philosophical scene. Since there were in philosophy no tempting physical applications or ingenious experimental tests whose devising could distract from theoretical inquiry, and since the ferment of religions, with none established or clearly dominant, kept pointing to theoretical issues, American philosophers were relatively free to be as theoretical as they wished. In the Classical Period, for special circumstantial reasons, it happened that two of the six men, Santayana and Whitehead, were born and largely educated in another country, four had a vivid awareness of religious values, while Santayana and Dewey were radical critics of all religion in anything like a conventional sense. One, James, was immersed at the outset of his career in the new science of psychology. Peirce was deeply versed in mathematics, several branches of physics, and the new science of symbolic logic, with some exposure to experimental psychology. Whitehead was a distinguished geometrician and contributor to theoretical physics, as well as a great logician. Dewey was an expert in the psychology of education, still another. Royce was one of the most profound students of German philosophy who has ever lived, in Germany or out of it. All six were deeply concerned with philosophical problems and more than superficially acquainted with the history and international status of these problems. These six men between them possessed an awareness of the intellectual landscape in some respects never before exhibited. Although each was intimately influenced by one or more of the others, yet not one is merely derivative, or anything like it. I submit that their equipment to deal with the totality of knowledge of their day was better, even considering how much more there was to know, than had been that of Hegel, Fichte, Schelling, Schopenhauer, and Nietzsche in Germany. The American group was, for the most part, in the middle of the problems produced by scientific advances, not on the periphery of them, but they were also richly sensitive to the religious and humanistic heritage going back to the Greeks. It was a golden opportunity, and I am convinced that it elicited some golden results, but we in this country are so modest that we look in awe to some venerable university abroad as if the refinement of its traditions guaranteed superior wisdom. I for one am not convinced that we have any less to give than to gain from interchanges with Europe or Britain, though I should be less sure of this had not one very great Englishman—so typically not English in many ways—thrown in his lot with us for a dozen grandly productive years.

To make the upsurge of American philosophy of the last one hundred years possible it was necessary that the base of philosophizing should be broadened to include more than politics, religion, and somewhat stale echoes of European science. Gibbs may have been the only great natural scientist of his day and country, but the northeastern

American universities began about that time to be alive with scientific activity. Two young men with philosophical inclinations, Charles Peirce and William James, were exposed early and intensively to this ferment. They were also brought up on religious interests, treated in a highly intellectual way, and with a noble trust in reason. A third, Royce, came under their influence and also under some of the influences which had molded them, but Royce added a grasp perhaps not surpassed in Germany itself of the philosophical tradition of that country, in which he was for years a student. All three men, indeed, were well aware of German—and James at least of French—thought. The German influence also came to the country through immigrants of philosophical gifts and in many other ways. This influence did not make the philosophy of this country a mere weakened echo of German idealism, for all of our principal philosophers were exposed, in a way no German is likely to be, to the entire force of the English tradition, with it ideals of clarity and sobriety. Thus, while Peirce apparently did his first careful philosophical reading in Kant, he also discussed the reasoning with his mathematician father, who showed him many logical flaws, and with Chauncey Wright, a scientist and vigorous disciple of John Stuart Mill, with whom he had 'daily' argument for years. Peirce, James and Royce gave the philosophy of this country a foundation as broad and deep as that which any country has ever had. I shall be accused of exaggeration, but not perhaps by those who know these men. In the past one hundred years there has, I think, been nothing in the world like the philosophical renaissance in the United States between 1865 and the present day in the high quality of imaginative philosophizing.

I also find that almost the entire gamut of philosophical problems confronting Western civilization has been centrally dealt with during the two or three centuries of philosophizing in this country, and that nearly all the important points of view have been represented, and well represented, by one or another of its philosophers. To survey the resources of philosophy generally one scarcely needs, any longer, to look across the Atlantic. There is somewhat more need to look across the Pacific, but there are competent Buddhist scholars among us also.

The most famous recent philosophical movements in Europe— Bergsonianism, existentialism, phenomenology, analysis—are not, one may suggest, so superior to the American classical philosophers as has been widely assumed. A great deal of Bergson, without his neglect of intellectual devices, is in James, Peirce, and Whitehead; Peirce might be called the first phenomenologist of all, and in some ways he remains still the best. James and especially Whitehead are rich in subtle phenomenological accounts. When Whitehead called metaphysics "a descriptive science," he meant that concepts are to be derived from concrete experience. As for sensitiveness to the central role of language in philosophy, Peirce in his theory of signs was in some ways at least the equal of Wittgenstein. He said, long before the latter, that the certainty of mathematics is a matter of our own sign-using conventions.

Even if my own efforts, including months of study with Husserl and Heidegger, to appreciate the continental and British achievements have been somewhat unsuccessful, so that my remarks in the previous paragraph require to be largely discounted, it still would not follow that the American movement deserved to be neglected. On the whole it has been just what those mentioned were not, at once daring and constructive, while yet concerned with canons of evidence and analytic clarity. The claim to have rendered obsolete all philosophical speculation, all metaphysics in the grand manner, may plausibly be made, but, I submit, it ought in honesty to test its case against the strongest, not the weakest, of recent representatives, those who combine the old imaginativeness and courage with adequate knowledge of modern logical techniques. These representatives have worked largely in this country rather than in Europe. It is quite obvious to that the most penetrating, imaginative, and yet careful, speculations of the last one hundred years have occurred here, not elsewhere. Wittgenstein may be subtler than anyone else as an unspeculative philosopher, though it might be hard to say what he sees that neither Peirce nor Dewey was aware of. Moore may have been a better man to scare a young student out of daring to speculate than we have had, though Lovejoy was searching, without wishing to scare anyone, but unless positivism or positivism plus a poetic existentialist anthropology, or plus a subtle theory of language in its more banal or harmless aspects—unless these are the precious gifts of philosophy, Europe has had little to offer of late. In any case, these things are now capably represented among us.

Has there been progress, in the sense of solutions to problems, in the course of our philosophical history? To answer this question is to declare one's own philosophy. I think that there are five major problems which have been pervasive from Edwards and Parker to Peirce and Whitehead, and that the treatment of these by the last two is incomparably more illuminating than that by earlier thinkers. This treatment is speculative, not positivistic or merely "therapeutic." The problems are solved, not dismissed or dissolved. It was Dewey who first said that philosophical problems are abandoned, not solved, but the Peirce-Whitehead theory of Creative Relativity positively solves problems. The almost innumerable writers who today deny the solubility of speculative puzzles, or who answer speculative questions by arguing that they need not arise if we are careful, do not know or understand this particular form of solution. If I am wrong, if the thing to do is to dismiss or avoid the questions, then there have been, or are, those among us who are capable of defending that position in one or another of its several forms. It is, however, amusing that British writers today seem almost unable to see that anything philosophical is going on here unless it be of the positivistic or therapeutic sort. It is true that we have fallen into a bit of a trough from the wonderful heights of the recent wave, but another wave may be forming.

The five speculative problems are: God and Cosmos, Mind and Matter, Freedom and Causality, Substance and Event, and finally a priori and Empirical knowledge (or Reason and Experience). One may add to these a sixth problem which practical or political rather than speculative, Equality and Sovereignty. The clue to the adequate philosophical illumination of this practical problem cannot be found, I believe, until we have gained some understanding of the theoretical ones.

At least the first four and the last of the six problems are fairly close to the surface from the beginning. All the colonial philosophers had much to say about God; Edwards had a radically idealistic theory of matter; he anticipated much that has been current lately concerning the alleged compatibility of moral freedom with strict causal determinism and argued this question at length and with great sharpness; he almost anticipated Whitehead's analysis of substance into an event-sequence, perhaps following some hints of Descartes. The fifth speculative problem, that of Reason and Experience, was sharply formulated by

Theodore Parker.

My view—naive enough, some will think—is that none of the problems were satisfactorily illuminated anywhere in the world in the seventeenth, eighteenth, or early nineteenth centuries, but that several of them at least can now be given a reasonable solution, thanks chiefly to the work of our 'Six Classical Philosophers,' especially Peirce and Whitehead—work chiefly written, though not always immediately published, between the years 1866 and 1933, that is during the last third of the nineteenth and the first third of the twentieth centuries. During the second third of our century, much good detailed work has been done, but in general not quite of a fundamental nature. We have been going through one of those skeptical eras, like that of the Second Academy, which may seem to themselves almost definitive, but which so far have always been followed by new outbursts of speculation. There are signs that anti-speculation will not be the last word this time either. It may not be amiss to take a good look at the overall adventure of American thought from Edwards to Dewey, so that we shall not perchance exchange our best inheritance for an inferior European product, or a superficial contemporary fashion.

Whether Europeans can profit by the study of our tradition is for them to consider. We learned from them for centuries; if they are too preoccupied, or for some other reason unable, to learn from us now, it is possibly their loss. It must be admitted that multitudes of young philosophers in this country today seem determined to Europeanize themselves as much as possible. The glamour of the old world, with its incomparable artistic riches, and its one time speculative grandeur, still fascinates. Perhaps it is for the best that it be so. We do not want to fall into mere provincialism ourselves, but our own tradition is at least worth a closer look than some of us appear to suspect.

That the foregoing talk of 'solving' speculative problems will sound quaint to many, I well know. Doubtless it is wise to take all such talk with considerable reserve, but the fashionable clichés about the essentially illusory nature of metaphysical ideas are, I am very sure, not nearer to literal correctness. We must, with Hume, and even more than Hume, be skeptical of our skepticisms, or we shall only be duped in a different way from the overconfident metaphysicians. Let it be not forgotten that Kant thought he knew exactly what were the limits of human knowledge or of humanly significant questioning. His work produced one of the maddest speculative outbursts of all. The wise balance here is not necessarily attained by giving free rein either to suspicion of, or to confidence in the human power to find rational overall meaning in life and the cosmos. Moore, Wittgenstein, Sartre, Heidegger, ably represent one extreme; but where in England, Germany, or France today are the able representatives of the balancing contrary attitude of speculative confidence? Heidegger never gets free of anthropomorphism, and even in his anthropology he eschews what most of us mean by rationality.

Whitehead's prophecy of thirty years ago is still plausible, that while Europe has lost her speculative freedom and courage, this country has not. The chief qualification to be added is that if the present trend away from our heritage were to go far enough, the Western world as a whole would be in the plight Whitehead saw Europe to be in. Let it not be so. The Western world needs all of its heritage to survive. Consider one of our now declining rivals, Marxist communism. Communism has offered an alleged solution to all of our six problems, and this claim is one of its assets. If we have no better solution, or no solution, this is scarcely a source of strength.

It is rather alarming that the communist solutions have been, to so large an extent, merely duplicated by many of our living free world philosophers. Of course a communist can be right, and indeed must be right in some beliefs, but consider this: the communist says, "the solution to the God problem is that 'God' stands for a superstition, encouraged by certain vested interests." Just so do many of us think. The communist says that mind is an emergent quality of certain material systems and that matter can exist in total independence of mind. Just so say many of us. The communist thinks, or at least does not clearly deny, that human liberty and strict causal regularity are compatible, and that moral freedom is the "acceptance of necessity," or at least, of the laws of nature This is today a fashionable philosophical position everywhere. The communist view concerning events and substances is perhaps less clear-cut; but similarly cloudy, and not significantly different, is the view held by many of us. The communist thinks that all knowledge is empirical, with an element of rational interpretation which is ultimately pragmatic, and this too is a favorite doctrine among us, so here are five speculative problems concerning which we apparently are scarcely wiser than the communists.

I believe that the communist is in serious error on all five topics, though least so in respect to the fourth, substances and events. I admit that there are some true insights, for instance "the transformation of quantity into quality" has a certain validity, but we have a vastly superior heritage than any communist is utilizing, and why should we not cultivate that heritage?

The value of reminding ourselves of our superior speculative insight is rather in the positive inspiration which it might furnish us and our friends. We cannot respond with a uniform generally accepted system of our own. Our method of freedom rules that out, but it might be well if many of us freely came to accept a system which carries thought to the highest level open to us. We believe that we have something precious to maintain, and yet mere political freedom seems not quite enough. I believe that the communist content is basically wrong at most points, but so may ours be if we do not take care.

Is there really no connection between our faith in the right not to be tyrannized over for the alleged benefit of future generations, as this benefit is defined by a ruling clique, and the belief that only one, namely God, has an unconditioned right to prefer His/Her wisdom to that of the rest of us? Has the definition of a liberal, one "who knows that he or she is not God," really been superseded? Or does it now mean "one who knows that there is or may be no God?" Is there not some loss of cutting edge with this shift? If there is a connection between human equality and the common immeasurable inferiority of all human beings to deity, then it might help our political idealism to arrive at the most enlightened view of deity which our history makes available.

Can faith in the value of freedom have simply no connection with superior insight into its universal metaphysical principle? If that principle is merely causality, then we have nothing to offer which has not been common property for more than two thousand years, but suppose the principle is the secularization of the theological ideas of creativity, of action which no causal explanation can ever derive from antecedent conditions, or of decision whose possibility can indeed be explained, but not the realization of precisely this possibility rather than others which would have been equally explicable from the same conditions.

Can our greater faith in the value of consciousness and ideas be simply unrelated to any superior insight into the cosmic role of the mind? If that role is to emerge from mere matter, that is, if mind is not of cosmic dimensions at all, then we can be no wiser than Marxists on the basic point. Suppose, however, mind really is the explanation of matter, as many great intellects, from Leibniz and Berkeley to Peirce and Whitehead, have held? Then it is we who are free to understand this.

Is it really likely that we shall make the most of our principle of the preciousness of individuality if we have no carefully conceived doctrine of the nature of enduring individuality in the stream of events connected together in space-time? Marxists mock our notion of soul or self, claiming that the social group is the enduring identity, not the person. If in reply we merely assert the individual against the group, then we are likely to fall into an anarchism no better than the collectivism we oppose and rather less realizable in practice. The Buddhists long ago rejected the 'soul,' but they did not fall into either anarchism or collectivism. Their wisdom at this point is essentially duplicated, more or less independently, by the 'Buddhisto-Christian' view of Peirce, and still more completely, and with improvements, by Whitehead's 'philosophy of organism.' Incidentally, it is worth noting that Emerson, Peirce, and Whitehead have had affinities—of which to some extent they have been conscious—with far Eastern thought.

Can mere empiricism give us a standard for judging the forces of history, and for distinguishing, however cautiously, tentatively, or roughly, between the ethical and the triumphant? Over a century ago Theodore Parker argued vigorously that religious and ethical first principles, like scientific ones, cannot be empirical. Royce continued the argument, and James unwittingly provided a brilliant example of the hopeless inconclusiveness of empiricism when applied to transempirical problems. Peirce, Whitehead and some more recent writers, have carried the analysis further.

The value which I have been imputing to recent speculative philosophy, chiefly American, though with partial analogues in Italy (Varisco), France (Lequier, Boutroux, Bergson, Le Ruyer), Germany (Fechner, Wenzl), and England (Ward, Alexander), and elsewhere, does not of course imply its acceptability as it stands. I shall mention four out of a number of respects in which I personally find it unsatisfactory. First, concerning the method and logical status of speculative philosophy: are its statements analytic, synthetic a priori, consequences of meaning postulates, phenomenological insights, or what? I find neither Peirce nor Whitehead sufficiently clear at this point, though not so unclear as many of their critics suppose. Second, though Whitehead seems to me to have come closer by far than any other metaphysician in the grand manner to ridding theistic philosophy of its well-known antinomies, nevertheless his exposition on this topic is marred by serious ambiguities and apparent or real inconsistencies, which suggest that he was groping toward a theory which he did not quite reach. In the last conversation which I had with him he indicated just that. If his view can be freed of these weaknesses, one may well put Whitehead above other great theistic philosophers, who have not even been in the neighborhood of a tenable theory of deity. The rest are all impaled upon the horns of ancient dilemmas which arise from their very principles. Whitehead's difficulty here arose, on the contrary, chiefly from his not quite adhering to his general principles when he came to the religious problem. He did not wander far from them either, but far enough to get into trouble, yet the remedy was in his own hands. This, though to a lesser extent, is also true of Peirce. It is not true of Augustine, Thomas, Spinoza, Kant, or Hegel.

Third, Whitehead's rather Platonic theory of 'eternal objects' seems to do insufficient justice to the case for a more nominalistic view, and is doubtfully consistent with the ultimacy assigned to process or 'creativity.' Peirce suggests a conception of the "evolution of the Platonic forms themselves" which may provide a clue.

Fourth, since Whitehead has ceased to write, new interests and new criteria have emerged in philosophy, for instance a new attention to the centrality of language in human thought. Everything has to be reconsidered in the light of these new preoccupations, but no recent work of high genius, such as scores of careful students have found Whitehead's to be, can be evaluated by a raising the of the eyebrows, whatever our remarkable contemporaries at Cambridge or Oxford may think. It needs to be reconsidered, yes, but reconsidering is still considering. The cultures of England and this country have by their confluence produced no greater joint product than Whitehead's vision of cosmic creativity. Even it, of course, is but a stepping stone; however, the claim of many to need no such stone will be more impressive when we see them reaching more exalted philosophical objectives without its aid than they are now contenting themselves with. I dare to say that one might about as easily reach great heights in philosophy without benefit of the work done in modern America as to reach them in physics without using the work of modern Germans. Is this statement extreme? If so, it can cause little harm. The most one can do with European provincialism, in which some citizens of the United States choose to participate, is to mitigate it ever so slightly. The economic bases of that provincialism alone seem to guarantee its persistence far into the future.

The vigor of the American philosophical development would not have been possible without careful consideration of the work of German, French, and British writers. We Americans have been in a position to travel, and to import foreign publications and foreign scholars, and we have not made it a point of honor to refuse to learn from these. This good fortune and this modesty are sources of strength. Our danger, however, has become an inverted snobbery, turned against our own past.

My proposal, then, is that philosophy in this country, not of course only here but particularly here has arrived at a metaphysics in which human freedom and human consciousness are given a congenial setting, unfavorable both to collectivism and to anarchic individualism, but favorable to reason in religion and religion in reason, and furnishing an ethical principle—not, of course, an ethical code—which is valid for all rational beings, independently of factual circumstances. Those of us who can accept this doctrine are in no danger of wondering what it is that our political freedom enables us to enjoy.

A philosophy of cosmic freedom and creativity can consistently exercise tolerance toward other philosophies, even those seeming to deny freedom, yet tragedy is logically inherent in a philosophy of freedom, such as Whitehead's. There can be no absolute harmonization of multiple freedom, even by divine 'persuasion,' not because God is weak but because it is meaningless to speak of absolute control over free beings. For a metaphysics of freedom, a simply 'unfree' being is also an incoherent notion; hence the notion of absolute control or absolute providential guarantee is logically, not just factually, vacuous. The higher the level of freedom, the greater the inherent risks of conflict as well as opportunities of valuable harmony. Thus, human life is bound to have aspects of great danger. How shall the miserably poor who now largely inhabit much of the world acquire some share in the wealth they see around them; and not someday, but soon? They refuse to wait. Our native optimism, not our best speculative philosophy, is at fault here. We did not believe that the dilemma of the all too even race between population and resources could be so desperate as the facts show it to be. Indeed, we all along refused to read Malthus intelligently and thereby lost a great opportunity to prepare ourselves for what is now upon us. Dewey, so far as I know, has ignored the Malthusian problem, and Peirce and Whitehead take it too lightly by far. Royce, the careful student of Hegel, ignored Marx, though surely Hegel's greatest contribution, for good or ill, was precisely his unintended part in the production of Marxism.

It is not that Whitehead, for instance, was committed to a sociopolitical or ethical code which is held to be uniquely fitting for all situations. Quite the contrary, he denies this, but he did not focus, as we need to, on certain tragic aspects of things: race prejudice, stubbornly persisting in all our cities in spite of rapidly rising consciousness of rights on the part of the victims, population increase beyond any comfortable possibility of production increase, and finally the grim dilemma, risk nuclear destruction. We still want a tragedy free, comfortable domestic existence. It cannot be. Individual self-interest is not an ultimate idea, for ultimately every individual perishes—and indeed everything we know will presumably perish—except God. Here is the genuine alternative to mere individualism. We have given it lip service, have not quite believed it. The "glory of God" is more literally the aim of existence in Whitehead's or Peirce's philosophy than in conventional Christianity.

The times which try people's souls also sift their philosophies. If I am right, suitable working ideas are in principle derivable from 'neoclassical metaphysics,' as I call it; but they need focusing on the actual needs and dangers.

Charles Hartshorne

THE IDEA OF CREATIVITY IN AMERICAN PHILOSOPHY

In the beginning, philosophy in the North American colonies was chiefly religious and political. The religious philosophy was Calvinistic, by which I mean that it was an argument for theological determinism. God's power and wisdom determine all things, including human choices. Human beings choose nothing except what God in eternity has decreed they shall choose. True, we may choose even to rebel against God, but only if God has decreed that we shall do just that. In spite of this divine responsibility for the rebellion, it was held to be quite appropriate for God to condemn the rebel to eternal damnation.

This strange doctrine was nowhere taken more seriously than in the colonies. Jonathan Edwards is the most famous, but not the sole, exponent of the view. His defense of theological determinism was skillful. Many recent defenders of determinism who do not share the religious faith of Edwards repeat, knowingly or not, some of his arguments. They share his conception of the meaning of freedom, that it is simply the ability to do what one wishes to do, unhindered by other individuals. When sinners rebel against God, God having decreed this rebellion, the sinners do what they really want to do. That God has made them such that they will want to do it makes no difference to the voluntary character of the act. It springs from the sinners' own will, and this is no less true because their will itself sprang originally from the divine will. Moreover, Edwards insists, we have no right to repudiate the principle of causality, according to which every event is the consequence of antecedent causes, so that, as we are born and as our environment is constituted, so we must act at every moment of life. If we repudiate causality then, it is argued, we cannot claim to know

69

God, the supreme cause of all things. We must use the idea of cause to arrive at knowledge of God, and we cannot have it both ways, we cannot cast away the ladder which takes us to the divine when we come to interpret our own place in the God created universe.

Today many secularists duplicate much of this reasoning without using the idea of God. They merely substitute science for the worship of God. We cannot have science without causality, they say, and we cannot accept causality in science and yet make an exception of ourselves. For there is a science of psychology. Heredity and environment determine actions. However, we are free in that we choose means to ends and act as we see fit, within such limits as are set by our social and political traditions. Free action is voluntary action, without undue interference from others. Many of my fellow philosophers are non-theistic Calvinists. If I find this somewhat amusing, it is doubtless because I am a theistic non Calvinist.

In political philosophy the colonists or some of them, were radical apostles of freedom. They held that political rights come from the people as a whole, not from divinely selected leaders. Calvinists themselves had much to do with this, for they practiced a sort of ecclesiastical democracy. No one knows if he or she is elected to salvation; each of us, for all one knows, is a condemned sinner. So let no one arrogate to self undue power over others. Thus, theological determinism appeared to fit political libertarianism well enough.

The reign of theological determinism was long lasting. Benjamin Franklin, while still a youth, wrote an essay in this vein. He was, however, too practical a man to be satisfied with a metaphysical paradox of this sort, and in his prime he ignored the question. An interesting case is Emerson, a writer who had a great influence upon my own youth. Emerson left the church, and by any normal standards was an unbeliever, or at least a good deal of a heretic. He was influenced by Hindu thought and professed a rather vague monism. But still, the Calvinist influence is readily detectable. Emerson was an explicit believer in determinism, and his conception of deity, which he called the "Oversoul," was of an all-determining spiritual order or Karma by which exact justice was done to all individuals. He wrote in his journal, "There is no chance, no anarchy. Every God is sitting in his sphere." What is this but a poetic echo of Calvinism? The world is completely under divine control, nothing happens at random, all is ordered by divine wisdom to the last detail. The proof that Emerson really meant this is found in what he set down in his diary some weeks after his small son died: "I comprehend nothing of this fact except its bitterness. Explanation I have none, consolation none that arises out of the fact itself; only diversion; only oblivion of this, and pursuit of new objects."

That we have here no mere momentary outpouring of unbearable grief is shown by his writing a year later: "I have had no experiences nor progress to reconcile me to the calamity . . . there should be harmony in facts as well as in truths. Yet these ugly breaks happen . . . which the continuity of theory does not contemplate."

It does not seem to occur to Emerson that discontinuity might have theoretical status as well as continuity. Why did he have to wait for his son's death to discover that misfortunes are no respectors of persons or their merits? As though the writer or writers of the book of Job, more than 2,000 years before, had not discussed this very question, not to mention the ancient Greek philosophers.

To be sure Emerson, as he confessed, was not a philosopher, but a poet, moralist, and essayist, who was under the spell of John Calvin, himself under the spell of Saint Augustine, who in turn was under the spell of Greek philosophy. It was the Greek philosophers—the materialist Democritus and the Stoics—who first worked out the deterministic theory for Europeans. Even theological determinism is essentially stoic. Augustine never genuinely freed himself from the fetters of Greek thought, nor did Emerson long afterwards.

The effective break with Calvinism, in the 1880s with Charles Peirce and William James. They were followed by John Dewey and the Anglo-American Alfred North Whitehead. Paul Weiss and many others are in this tradition. At least one of the deists of the revolutionary period, Ethan Allen, who was a military general and a philosopher—one of the rather few people in history who have been both—gave an eloquent defense of theological indeterminism. He thought the Calvinistic doctrine was absurd, even comic.

The last gasp of the Stoic-Calvinist view may be seen in Josiah Royce. Royce is perhaps closer to the Stoics than were Calvin or Augustine, for like his Stoic predecessors he identified God with the soul of the universe of which the human soul was a part or element. The view is still Calvinistic, for our choices are also God's choices; all the goods and evils in the cosmos, including our most wicked acts, are eternally chosen by the absolute will. Why then the many evils? Royce says the divine wisdom sees them as necessary to the good of the whole, but then wickedness cannot really be wickedness, since the wicked persons do exactly what God wills done. Royce tries to make sense out of this paradox. The wicked ones serve God's purpose all right, but, unlike the good ones, do not intend to do so. They do the right thing only in spite of themselves, whereas the good ones want to do good. Here Royce overlooks an obvious objection, "Why does it matter that the evil persons do not intend to do good, if they do it?" After all, even bad intentions, like all things else, are divinely chosen and do good. So they too cannot really be bad. Thus, there is no evil at all. All moral choice then must be meaningless since anything that can possibly happen is bound to be exactly what infinite wisdom selects for the perfection of the whole.

I regard Royce as the end of a blind alley, an alley into which the Stoics and Augustine led Western religious thought. Fortunately some of our recent philosophers have presented an alternative, perhaps nowhere else in the world quite so clearly worked out. In the development from William James and Charles Peirce through Dewey to Whitehead, I see one of the longest steps forward ever taken in the philosophy of religion. I shall try to sketch this development.

To William James, as to some European philosophers, especially French, it seemed obvious that the mere absence of external coercion, or even of internal compulsion in the form of ungovernable passion, madness, drunkenness, or other psychological abnormality, is not the whole of our moral freedom. Something has been left out, and this something is the heart of the matter. The essential point is the power to decide or determine the previously undecided or indeterminate. James analyzed this power in various ways. From a religious standpoint the issue is this: does God make our decisions for us by creating us and our world just as we and the world are, or does God decide only some features of the creation, leaving it to us to decide others? Are we or are we not, with God, in however humble a fashion, creators as well as creatures? If God is the sole creator and we mere creatures, then not only are we radically inferior to God; we are simply nothing at all, so far as creativity is concerned. If supreme reality is supreme creativity, what can lesser forms of reality be if not lesser forms of creativity? James felt deeply that we must be creators as well as creatures. The notion that God's eternal plan settles everything seemed to him to contradict our sense of being agents of decisions. Some things are for us to settle, and it is nonsense to say this and also to say that God in eternity settles everything.

What is it to create? James was clear about this. It is to produce a definite actuality out of antecedent somewhat indefinite possibility. The future, he held, is partly ambiguous or indeterminate, not simply for our knowledge but in itself or objectively as future. Only when no longer future is an event fully defined. The future consists not merely of what will happen but of what may or may not happen, depending upon the choices of creatures. We help to define the world. No deity has given it complete definition once for all. This is the dignity of being human, that we are in our humbler fashion co-creators with deity. One can read a hundred essays by determinists and scarcely find one which shows understanding of this claim. For example, many writers talk as though the objection to determinism were only that causally determined choices could not be voluntary, and hence, for instance it would be absurd to punish criminals. James laughs to scorn the notion that the issue hangs upon how criminals are to be treated. Of course, he says, a determinist can defend punishment if he or she can show that the fear of punishment deters from crime. Who could be so stupid as to be unable to see this. James was thinking in religious and ethical, not in legal, terms. He was perfectly aware of the difference between unconstrained, reasonable, actions, and coerced or half mad ones. This was just not the contrast which primarily concerned him. His question was, "Do we help to create or determine the world, or is it fully determinate already by cause in being before we were born? Did the first dawn of creation write what the last day shall read, or is the world still in the making so that new causal factors, our decisions among them, keep entering the stream of events."

Charles Peirce, a friend of James, and a great mathematical and logical genius—also an experimental scientist-physicist, astronomer, and even psychologist—decided, when about forty years old, that determinism was a mistaken doctrine, and mistaken from a scientific point of view. His concern was not, as was that of William James, primarily with our moral freedom, or with psychology, but with physics and cosmology. His aim was broader than that of fitting humanity into the scheme of things. He wanted to understand the very meaning of causality and natural law. A radical evolutionist, he applied the notion of development to law itself. Natural laws are the habits of natural things; the most basic laws are the habits of the most fundamental sorts of things, such as atoms or light rays. The lesson of Darwinism, adequately generalized, is that species or natural kinds, and hence their habits, evolve and change slowly through time. Habits, being adaptations, are never absolutely rigid. There are always small deviations, chance variations. For this and other reasons Peirce adopted indeterminism not simply with respect to human beings or moral choices but with respect to all nature. Human freedom was a highly special case and no more. Boutroux in France had already hinted at such a view, but Peirce worked it out more explicitly.

Peirce called his doctrine, Tychism, from the Greek word for chance. Chance is real, in the form of slight deviations from any strict law or natural habit. Like James Clerke Maxwell, the last century's greatest physicist, Peirce took seriously the introduction into physics of the statistical conception of natural laws. Laws are averages, not absolute rules for the individual case. As a mathematician and physicist, he knew well what this meant, and he knew that no observations could possibly establish absolute or non statistical laws. At most, he pointed out, we can show that deviations from our scientific formulae, our statements of law, are not large, but from the statement, "the deviations are less than a certain small value," the statement "the deviations are exactly zero," i.e., nonexistent, does not in the least follow, even with probability. Quite the contrary, since zero is but one of an infinity of possible left open by observation, the probability that the value is strictly zero is as one to infinity. This, I maintain is a powerful argument, and it precedes quantum mechanics by several decades. Quantum mechanics has merely added the additional argument that not only can we not narrow possible deviations down to zero, we cannot even reduce them below a certain finite quantity. As a result determinism, so far from being a result of scientific observations already made, is shown to be in principle forever beyond the reach of observation, since it cannot even be approached asymptotically.

Chance, Peirce remarks, is in itself a negative idea, meaning absence of any necessity or strict law, but there is a positive side. In ourselves we experience deviation from habit as spontaneity, self-determination. Our existence, from the inside or for ourselves, consists of spontaneous feeling more or less illuminated by thought or the use of signs. Wherever habit is absolute or nearly absolute, thought and even feeling tends to lapse. It revives when habit fails to fit and something unhabitual must be done. Nowhere in nature, however, according to Peirce's doctrine, is habit or law literally absolute, hence nowhere is feeling altogether absent. The atoms in themselves consist of feelings with some slight degree of freedom or, to use Peirce's word, spontaneity. Nature consists of spontaneous or slightly free processes of feelings, which on higher levels reach the character of conscious thought.

An odd feature of Peirce's view is that he thought laws, though not holding absolutely, are evolving toward absoluteness. Nature is slowly becoming more habit ridden, and in the infinitely remote future it must fall into complete rigidity. Since this means the lapse of all feeling, and feeling is the very stuff of which reality is composed, it seems that nature is heading toward its own collapse into nothingness. The evolutionary process may then begin over again. Thus, time perhaps is circular in a strange fashion.

John Dewey was largely interested in social and political problems, rather than in individuals taken one by one as was James, or in the physical universe as was Peirce. Dewey agreed with James and Peirce that causal laws are not absolute and especially with the view of James that man is genuinely creative in a partly unfinished universe. The ambiguities of the future are real, objective; and life consists in progressive resolutions of these ambiguities. Dewey has a very sharp sense for a fundamental truth, as I view it, the truth that a human being is not ultimately a spectator of things, past, present, and future, but a maker of new forms of reality. The question is not so much, what is going to happen, that is a mere spectator's question, but rather, toward what outcome do we decide to bend our efforts. Until we decide there is, insofar, no definite future fact to behold; and after we decide it is the past we are contemplating not the future, so far as that decision is concerned. There is no time to rest in mere contemplation, even in the past, for each moment new decisions must be made. Taken as a whole every experience is decisive, active, rather than contemplative; contemplation is a partial aspect only. How we interpret the facts contemplated is really what use we make of then in the moment to moment process of decision making. There is no escape from deciding, except by lapsing into total unawareness; the idea of pure contemplation is an illusion, an attempted evasion of life's obligations. We may meet the obligations feebly, but meet them we must. Thinking is a form of living, and living is solving problems as to what to do next. Truth, reality, all basic concepts, must be interpreted in the light of this problem solving character of life.

I sympathize with much of what Dewey says. I quarrel only with what seem to me exaggerations or arbitrary restrictions in his account. First, he seems almost to deny that we can contemplate at all, even with respect to the past, or with respect to eternal characters of reality, which are common to past and future. It is never really clear how far he admits that the past, at least, is quite definite. Second, Dewey refuses to generalize his account of human nature into an account of nature at large. He has a dualistic cosmology, without quite admitting it. Is problem solving restricted to human beings or at least to the higher animals, or is something analogous pervasive of nature? Is experiencing, enjoying, suffering, peculiar to animals, or is something like it found in the very atoms?

Dewey denies this, but his reasons for the denial are quite unclear to me. I even wrote him about it once, but could not understand his answer. Third, Dewey refuses to admit any form of awareness superior to the human. He quarrels with belief in God on the ground that if all possible value is eternally in God then our existence adds nothing and is pointless, but he fails to note that note that some of us who believe in God do not say that all possible value is timelessly possessed by God; on the contrary, we say that God is perfect once for all only in certain abstract respects, and that the concrete values of the divine life are endlessly enriched by the creaturely lives. Dewey's own colleague at Barnard College of Columbia University, W. P. Montague, held this view, yet Dewey ignores the doctrine, save for one vague and careless remark which might possibly refer to it.

Whitehead agrees with his American predecessors concerning the basic distinction between the settled past and the indeterminate future, and, although without knowing it until near the end of his career, he agrees with Peirce that this distinction expresses a universal character of nature. He agrees also with Peirce that the inner aspect of the process of decision by which the unsettled future turns into the settled past is feeling always more or less tinged with thought or consciousness. In much of nature thought is at a minimum, but feeling is on all levels, atomic, molecular, cellular, animal. The only strictly insentient things are composites, for example swarms of atoms or molecules in a gas, or colonies of cells in a tree. Here Whitehead returns to the great thought of Leibniz: the notion of mere dead matter is due to the grossness of our sense perceptions. If we could see atoms or cells as individuals we should not think of them as mere dead matter, mere lumps of passive stuff, for we should observe their incessant and rhythmical activities.

A tree, said Whitehead once, is a democracy—he meant, a democracy of cells. Of course the tree does not feel, neither does a swarm of bees. It is the bees, not the swarm—it is the cells, not the tree—which feel. Only in animals with nervous systems do we meet with cell colonies that are more than that, each colony also an integrated individual acting and feeling as one. Whitehead has a carefully conceived, though not detailed, theory of how the nervous system makes this possible.

Perhaps Whitehead's greatest contribution is his analysis of the idea of creativity. To my mind his account is at this point much more penetrating than that of William James, or indeed anyone else before or since. Creativity, according to this account, belongs to the very essence of experiencing as such. To experience is to create, to create is to experience. Consider any momentary experience in its full concreteness, not just the sensory aspects or just the intellectual or emotional ones, but all aspects (e.g., your experience now). In this experience there is memory of what you have just previously experienced less than a second before. There are probably also visual and auditory perceptions, various thoughts, and many other features, yet all this is but one momentary experience. It is not a mosaic but a unitary reality, though with diverse aspects. This unitary reality is a creation. It must be, since it did not exist previously, and it is no mere rearrangement of things previously existent.

Once more, it is not a mosaic, a mere composite of things experienced, but a single experience of these many things. The one subject or momentary experience has many objects, past experiences remembered, parts of the body felt, ideas entertained, but these many things are now held in a new unity. "The many become one and are increased by one." The experience itself is as unitary as any of its objects—for example, as the just preceding experience which it remembers. since the new unity is not something previously there, and is no mere rearrangement of the things previously there, what can it be but a new creation? Could the previous multitude of things, such as parts of the body, causally dictate their own inclusion into a new thing? A causal law might tell us that some objects would be experienced more prominently than others, or more agreeably than others, and so on, but all this is abstract, and could apply to any number of conceivable experiences, as well as to just this unique one that occurs. We have the antecedent objects plus the law; out of this multiplicity we have to get a new object. A creative fiat is needed to weld the objects in conformity with the law into a new object.

Like Bergson, some of whose writings he had read long before, Whitehead sees that the essential creative art, basic to all others, is the art of experiencing. The most concrete form of beauty is a harmonious experience. In this sense we are all artists in every instant, more or less successfully creating beauty. The basic freedom is just the freedom to experience, to enjoy ever new states of feeling and thought, none with any possible duplicate in all the universe, and each experience has some aspect of beauty, since beauty is unity in contrast, and any experience is such a unity.

Creativity, thus conceived, is self-creation, and what are we concretely but experiencing individuals whose characters are largely the result of past experiences, each of which as a unitary whole was self-determined? "Freedom of Choice" in the practical or moralistic sense of choosing to 'do' this instead of that with our bodies and instruments is a secondary aspect or product of the primary freedom to experience a given situation in a fashion not dictated by the situation, even if one's own past is taken as part of the situation.

If the essential creativity is self-creativity, what becomes of the idea of one individual creating another? It is relativized, rather than simply denied. "The many become one and are increased by one" implies that each new synthesis of the many into one produces an additional item in the many and hence contributes to all subsequent self-creation. Your neighbors, so far as they perceive or know your experiences, will take them into their own experiences. You will thus have created something of their natures as well as something of yours. All creation is first of all self-creation, but since self-creation through perception draws upon antecedent cases of self-creation in others, all self-creation is also creation by others and of others. This is not a creation of others in the absolute sense, which would contradict their being truly self-creative, but only in a relative sense. Absolute creator on one side and absolute or merely passive creature on the other is a formula with no admissible meaning in Whitehead's philosophy. Calvinism is here refuted in the most radical fashion conceivable. No God could simply 'make' our experiences, for an experience has to be self-made, even though out of antecedent materials.

Whitehead has a deeply religious feeling about this matter. God does not coerce, and coercion has no absolute meaning in this philosophy. Coercion in the usual human sense is but an indirect form of power. Human tyrants or coercive agents force me to make a certain decision by threatening or injuring my body, or the bodies of those I care about; they do not directly influence my thought or will by this thought. God, however, has direct power over all creatures, dealing directly with all minds. How can God do this? In the Whiteheadian philosophy, nothing can influence the becoming of any experience save the things already there to be experienced. So God influences our experiencing if, and only if, in some not necessarily conscious way, we experience this thought or feeling. What is given in an experience as datum, conscious or not conscious, influences that experience; nothing else does.

For example, if my body influences my visual experience, this means that the optical system is directly felt. That we do not think of the data of vision as bodily but as things outside our skins is explained by genetic psychology, of which Whitehead worked out his own version. It is interpretation, thoroughly learned in infancy, which turns bodily processes directly experienced into the seeing of objects out there before us, vision apart from interpretation, or as sheer givenness, is, according to Whitehead, as bodily as pain, but as interpreted in adult life it is at the opposite extreme. Only in early infancy is the interpretation minimal or nonexistent, so that the experience is then, perhaps, merely bodily.

That God influences us at all times means that, as we always feel our bodies without necessarily thinking about them, so we always feel God; but here for the most part with still less conscious interpretation. Why, however, do we feel either the body or God? What forces us to do so? Simply that these objects offer us irresistible values. From our bodies we derive sensory qualities without which our experiences must be but empty or abstract outlines; from God we derive a basic guidance without which we would be living in a lawless chaos. The laws of nature are not mere habits of natural things, they are divinely inspired habits. Without this inspiration things could not coexist, for their self-creativity would be without a common direction. They would be like a vast committee with no chairman. Without commonly accepted rules, a world of mutually harmonious but self-determined processes is impossible. How are the rules to be established? Any rules are arbitrary, since there is no one possible world order but innumerable possible orders. There has therefore to be a decision, "let these be the rules." The decision can only be made by a single decider, whose influence upon the others is uniquely pervasive. This is Whitehead's theory of natural laws; they are divinely decided and the decision universally accepted since it offers each creature its only chance to belong to a cosmos rather than a chaos.

As Whitehead puts it, God 'persuades' the world, but does not coerce it. What God offers is indispensable and hence irresistibly attractive to all.

There are two important qualifications: the divine persuasion furnishes rules for the self-creation of creatures, but no rule can fully specify a single instance of such self-creation. Finally, each momentary experience must determine itself. Thus, though the world is not a chaos, an element of chance (Peirce) or anarchy remains. There is some degree of genuine disorder. That no conflict or evil should result is infinitely unlikely. This is not weakness on God's part, for the very purpose of the rules is to make freedom, with all its risks, possible. The risks are the price which must be paid for the opportunities which freedom alone can actualize. The further qualification, which is more difficult to explain, is that the more highly conscious creatures, such as ourselves, not only are free to get into conflict with one another in some degree, but are free to rebel in a measure against the divine persuasion, free to sin. Whitehead tries, in one chapter, to show how this possibility arises. It is the old theological problem, not of evil in general, but of moral evil. Mere suffering, aesthetic evil is not especially mysterious in his philosophy, for if there is self-determination everywhere the wonder is not that discord appears here and there, but that there is any harmony at all. The multiplicity of self-determining beings explains natural evil. Only God explains natural good. Moral evil remains somewhat puzzling. Part of the trouble here is perhaps that moral evil is so close to us that we can scarcely think disinterestedly and honestly about it.

A surprising feature of Whitehead's philosophy is its affinity, in certain aspects, with Buddhism. The Buddhists very early broke with the almost universal concept of individual substance, soul, or ego. For Buddhism, the reality of the individual is in the successive states, mental or bodily. As conscious, the individual is the experience. Strictly speaking, I am a new self each moment. Not only this, but by identification with others through love or compassion I am not simply distinct from other selves. Self-identity through time is not absolute, I both am and am not the one I was yesterday. Nonidentity with other human beings is also only relative, I both am and yet am not my neighbor. In this way, among others, the Buddhist seeks to subdue egoism. There is no point in relating actions to self-interest, rather than altruism, for selves have no absolute sameness through time and no absolute otherness in space.

All this can be translated into Whitehead's system. Each moment I am a new experience—Whitehead calls it a new "actual entity," or a new "occasion of experience." Each actual entity is self-created, a synthesis into which the previous experiences which I call mine enter in the form of conscious or unconscious memories, but many other actualities also enter, among them what I perceive or understand as the experiences of other human beings. Thus, my present reality is made up partly of my past reality and partly of the past realities of many other individuals. My unity with my own past is only relatively different from my unity with the past of my neighbors, friends, enemies, the constituents of my own body, and so on. Quite literally I am now both what I have been and, in lesser degree, what others have been. I am myself, but I also am other selves. There is relative separation from my past, and relative union with your past.

Whitehead draws from this the same conclusion that the Buddhists did from their rather similar doctrine, egoism, self-interest taken as the central motivation, is based upon an illusion, the illusion that each of us is a simply identical entity through time and a simply different entity from the others around us in space. Whitehead once in a lecture expressed this point in a whimsical fashion reminiscent by its very whimsicality of Zen Buddhism. "I sometimes think," he said, "that all modern immorality is due to Aristotle's theory of substance." A Buddhist would be more likely to understand this than anyone else.

The rejection of substance, of an identical entity, distinct for each human individual, simply one with itself, simply not one with any other self, is regarded as depriving selfishness of an illusory metaphysical support. "I love myself," says the believer in substance, "of course, for I am myself." If I love you, however, that is very different indeed, for I am not you at all. Thus, self-love is taken as metaphysical self-explanatory and love of others as metaphysically paradoxical. As psychologists tell us, however, self-love and love of others, like self-hate and hatred of others, are akin. There is no absolute or metaphysical gulf between them. According to Whitehead, self-love has essentially the same structure as love of others.

The present actuality is a synthesis of past actualities, some of which belong to the personal history of the particular human body to which the present experience is attached, and some of which do not, but this is a secondary distinction. The primary point is that a novel unit of experience unites in itself previous units. Your past and my past are both in my present on metaphysically the same terms, whatever differences of degree there may be. As for the future, if I take an interest in what I anticipate as my experiences tomorrow and am moved to take steps that they shall be agreeable experiences, I can in much the same way take an interest in what I anticipate as your experiences tomorrow and take steps that they shall be agreeable. There are no absolute but only relative differences in the two cases. I am of the opinion that Whitehead's doctrine has whatever merit the Buddhist doctrine has, plus considerably greater clarity and consistency, but of course Whitehead had the advantage of more than a thousand years of intellectual progress and the stimulus of Western science and logic.

Did Whitehead learn anything from the Buddhist psychology? The evidence is insufficient to answer this question. He mentions Buddhism a couple of times, but not with reference to their psychology, or their rejection of substance. My guess is that Whitehead reached the Buddhist insights independently, for he was wont to state his indebtedness, but it remains possible that there was an influence of which he happened not to be conscious. Whitehead's philosophy is the first great speculative system in the West which duplicates, in rather intimate fashion, the Buddhist relativizing of substantial identity and nonidentity of persons and, particularly, the Buddhist conviction that in the rejection, of soul-substance and of substance generally there is positive spiritual value. This is no reluctant abandonment or subordination of the notion of substance on the ground of insufficient evidence. This is rather a joyful rejection of an obstacle to spiritual fulfillment, the transcendence of a specious metaphysical basis of selfishness. It is the overcoming of the false and harmful absolutizing of essentially relative identities and differences. There is nothing like this in previous European thought, but there is something quite a good deal like it in much Asiatic thought originating in India.

Charles Hartshorne

FREEDOM, INDIVIDUALITY, AND BEAUTY IN NATURE

Science appears to banish freedom from the world. For science seeks causal laws, to which there are to be no exceptions. Given an actual situation, the laws should make the outcome of the situation inevitable. The most that freedom, in these terms, can mean is that the individual knows what he or she is doing, that here is no compulsion from without; and yet, nevertheless, the conditions within and without the individual, together with the causal laws, make the selection of a certain mode of acting inevitable. Many philosophers, living and dead—for example, the ancient Stoics—have held that this is all that anyone means, or needs to mean, by freedom. Yet some of us find this view unconvincing. We think that freedom must mean more than this; it must mean the psychological capacity, in the given case, of choosing any one of several courses of action. If we are right, is there not a conflict between freedom and the scientific point of view?

A second idea which often seems to fare badly at the hands of science is that of the uniqueness of the individual. Science, it seems, cannot deal with the unique, as such. Its laws do not state that this or that individual will behave thus and thus; but rather that any individual of a certain type, say a body with a mass of two pounds, moving with velocity of one hundredth of the speed and light, will under certain conditions proceed in such and such a manner, or produce such and such consequences. The individual is here a mere example of laws, and is never indispensable. Other individual would illustrate the same laws just as well. Perhaps the total cosmos is indispensable; but it is a question how far we can really know the cosmos as a whole, in its evolution through vast ages

Science also appears to banish beauty from the world, except as a merely human sentiment. The physicist or biologist does not ask: how beautiful is it? but: how does it behave? Science puts values aside, and its success has been without doubt largely owing to this renunciation. And yet, science itself is nothing save so far as it has value. And also, who would want to live if nothing seemed beautiful in the world? Then too, the greater the scientist, the more likely he or she is to regard the truths discovered as exhibitions of aspects of cosmic beauty, previously hidden from humanity.

I wish to consider these three problems of freedom, individuality, and beauty in the light of some adventure of my own as an amateur scientist. For many years I have been attempting to study the phenomenon of bird song scientifically. Bird song may always have appeared to us as more or less beautiful. But is it, one wonders, beautiful to the bird themselves? The science of biology has reason to take the question seriously. For the evolutionary account seeks to explain higher forms of life as further developments of tendencies found already, even in the lowest forms. Should we not then expect to find that the human sense of beauty has its forerunners in other animals? And where in nature, if not in birds, could we expect to find a primitive sense of the beauty of musical sounds? Certain birds produce sound patterns much more like human music than do any of the other lower animals. Many birds also display keen interest in sounds, as is proven, for instance, by their tendency to imitate them. Cats never pay our voices the compliment of imitation. They do not care that much about sounds. However, birds also learn unmusical sounds at times. So perhaps a sense of beauty has nothing to do with it? After long searching, I began, some years ago, to see how the facts might be made to answer the question: is there a primitive form of musical feeling in birds? If this could be shown, then we would know that the sense of beauty is not confined to us. It turned out, happily, that some of this evidence was also relevant to the question of freedom and individuality in nature. I shall try to sketch some of these findings.

If biology is to deal objectively with the question of a sense of beauty in animals, it must learn a lesson from students of human reactions to beauty. Writers on aesthetics agree that there is little to be gained by discussing the bald question: is this beautiful or is it not? There are so many kinds and degrees of beauty, or of aesthetic value. Some works of art are not exactly beautiful, but rather, pretty, sublime, amusing, expressive, and what not. And there are degrees of beauty, and of these other categories. One needs to be specific, and to ask—in what respects, how much, and by what standard, is a thing aesthetically good. Forty years of reflecting upon beauty in bird song have led me to adopt six standards for rating singers: first, loudness (or power); second, scope (or variety and complexity); third, continuity (the opposite of which is singing in little snatches, say of two seconds, broken by pauses three to ten times as long); fourth, purity of tone ("flute-like" or "bell-like," as ornithologists often say); and fifth, unity or musical pattern including such arrangements of notes as trills, accelerandos, crescendos, harmony and so on. Our five criteria are then: loudness, scope, continuity, purity of tone, unity. It is easy to see that we rate human music by similar criteria. Under each of the five variables, one can acknowledge in birds perhaps as many as eight differences of degree, from 1 to 9. We can then rate a song by five figures say 99866, that is, 9 points in loudness and scope, 8 in continuity, 6 in purity of tone, 6 in unity of pattern. In this way, the question becomes one of fact, is a relatively definite objective sense. The figures mentioned are about those that fit mockingbird. No one can rate the loudness of the mockingbird as much less than 9, for it can heard nearly as far as any bird of that size. The scope is also scarcely surpassed by any other bird, and the continuity is high, though not quite equal to the skylark and a few others. But the purity of tone is uneven, and never nearly equal to the wood thrush, for instance. And the unity of effect is likewise only fair, since the bird rambles from one little group of sounds to another, with somewhat loose connection between successive groups or stanzas. I also take into account a sixth criterion, imitative capacity, and under it allow points from 1 to 5. The mockingbird ranks 4th here. This makes up for its defect in tone and unity, and gives it about the same score as the thrush, or a total score of about 42 or 43. This is out of a possible 50, or 85% of perfection.

We have now turned our question of the aesthetic quality of songs into one of observable fact. How shall we test the proposition that the resulting ratings have biological significance, that they express differences, not only for human observers, but for birds? One way is to ask whether birds which sing better, that is, rate higher on our six-number system, also spend more of their time singing. For the more time a bird spends on this activity, the more important it must be for its mode of life. And if those for whom singing is most important do it best by our human standards, then this shows that these standards have biological significance, and are also, in some sense, the birds' standards. For quantity of singing is an objective fact about the birds themselves. Observation so far seems to show that in every region that has been carefully studied, the greatest quantity of singing per year is done by singers which are also high in their six-point rating. And the singers which sing the least in the year rate low. How could you explain this except by supposing that species for whom song is unimportant do not need to develop so much musical taste or skill as the others, since it is a secondary matter to them, a casual affair, with the main energies and interest elsewhere? So they demand less of themselves, and evolution provide with less ability in this respect. But the standards of ability are essentially the same with us, only are an immense distance behind us, at least in the complexity of musical patterns which they can execute or enjoy.

Another line of evidence is the following. All artists, and persons aesthetically sensitive avoid monotony, the direct repetition of the same thing over and over. As a writer on music has said, an art product falls between two unaesthetic extremes, chaos and mechanism. So do bird songs, especially those occurring in the sub-order of birds which is technically called Songbirds, the group *passeres* or *oscines,* in scientific Latin; these being the ones with highly developed organs of sound-production. The proof for this proposition is objective and statistical, and it is this: On the one hand singing birds repeat recognizable, musically coherent phrases or songs, and thus exhibit organization in their utterances. Songs are not bits of chaos. But on the other hand, it is equally true that the repetition is not mechanical; the extreme of monotony is avoided no less universally than that of mere randomness. To have discovered this is my greatest piece of luck in this business. I got to it by reflecting upon the apparent monotony in the singing of many species; the same little song over and over, hundreds or thousands or times, in one day. Does this not show, I asked myself, that the artist's sensitiveness to monotony is wholly lacking in birds? The clue to the answer came from the remarkable fact that the birds which sing the same song over and over have much longer pauses between songs, than those which sing a variety of songs in turn. In other words, the versatile, non-repetitive singers sing more continuously, with shorter pauses between songs or phrases. Variety and continuity are positively correlated. Thus we have two extreme types of singers (with of course intermediate cases): at one extreme, those, like the mockingbird, which sing many different phrases, limiting repetition to a few reiterations, and avoid the pauses which are so conspicuous a feature of the other style of singing. But why not two further styles: versatile or repetitious without pauses; and non-repetitious but with pauses? Logically these types are just as possible as the other two. But they scarcely occur among Songbirds anywhere in the world, so far as I know. On the assumption that birds have a musical sense, this is what we should expect. No musician would repeat a phrase or short song over and over without pause, for it would be intolerably monotonous; but a musician who knew but one song might well repeat it many times, only he would pause long enough between repetitions so that it would seen fresh each time. With creatures living in a narrow present, so that only the very near past is vividly in mind, a rather short pause would suffice to prevent the impression of monotony. But some pause there must be, with repetitious singing if there is any sense of the past, and any sensitivity to monotony. So the facts fall into line. Note that this theory meets the usual scientific test that it give us power to predict. I can predict that in any new region to which I may go, I will find some birds with little variety between their successive utterances but relatively long pauses (several times the length of the songs of phrases); and other birds with middling variety, and for minutes at a time, scarcely any pauses. I can also predict that there will <u>not</u> be birds without variety and yet with very short pauses, nor will there be birds with great variety and long pauses. Thus the scientific theory, that it could be falsified by some conceivable observation, is met. One could easily observe the types of songs which our theory forbids, should they occur. But they do not. Apparent exceptions are statistically insignificant, and in good part can be fairly explained as compatible with the theory. Above all, they are negligible in number, compared to the quantity of songs which fit the theory.

Now we come to the question of freedom. The fact is that the higher the rating of songs, the less predictable they usually are in detail. Songs with much scope of variety usually involve a number of phrases of patterns which follow each other in a free, rather than fixed, order. No amount of observation will tell you which phrase is to come next. Also it will not tell you, in the case of repetitious singing with long pauses, just <u>how</u> long a given pause will last, for this varies somewhat each time. It is thus as though the bird with pauses had to decide in each case when to resume, and as though the bird with a repertoire of different phrases had to decide each time which out of its bag of tricks to select. In this unpredictability I see the freedom of the bird. Determinists may reject this interpretation, and may say: the unpredictability is relative to our ignorance of the factual conditions in and around the bird. Of course they can say this. But can they <u>know</u> that the conditions, if known, would make the outcome predictable? Or is this merely dogma? True, they may say that my idea of freedom is only a dogma. I have an answer to this, but there is not enough time for it here. I am content to remark that, no only do we not <u>now</u> know any law by which the birds' behavior in the respect mentioned would become predictable, from the conditions, as we human beings can observe them, but we could not reasonable hope to find such a law. For laws, as we can verify and use them, are bound, at least on this level, to be statistical only; so that we should at most be able to say that, <u>usually</u>, under such and such conditions the bird will sing phrase B after phrase A, rather than phrase C or D, or will <u>usually</u> pause approximately six seconds rather than five or seven. Thus not only does our science as it is now permit is to suppose that the individual bird is free, but our science, as it can be expected to become, will continue to do so. If in physics the three-body problem is only roughly manageable, we are never going to have absolute prediction of how a vertebrate animal will act, for the complexity is here enormous. Thus the concept of freedom can never be ruled out on the basis of scientific results.

Listen to one of the Carolina wrens: it makes up a song by reiterating some little phrase several times in quick succession, say four times: "tea-kettle, tea-kettle, tea-kettle, tea-kettle" or "How is Teaver, how is Teaver, how is Teaver, how is Teaver." Then it pauses several seconds, and repeats. But note what soon happens: the number of "tea-kettles" drops from four to three, or rises to five. You can predict, with some assurance, that one of these changes will soon happen. But will the change be from four down to three, or up to five? And just how many fours will intervene before the next three or five occurs? I call this practice, which many birds indulge in, "juggling with numbers." We have experimental evidence that birds can distinguish between three, four, and even six, successive sounds. So you must not say that the bird merely cannot count. Rather, being sensitive to monotony, it avoids too constant persistence in a given number. An individual wren also has a repertoire of distinct song. Since each song has at least three numbers, if the individual has a dozen songs, there are thirty-six variations. At a given moment, any one of the thirty-six could be used. One can conceive probability laws here, but not definite individual predictions genuinely justified by knowledge.

What we seem to have shown is this: the evolution of singing, from an unimportant, exceptional activity, to a large portion of the bird's living, is also an evolution toward aesthetic quality, even by our human standards. And it seems to be an evolution toward freedom in the sense of decisions unpredictable because they are creative acts of determining what otherwise is open, indeterminate. Bird song is a fine symbol of what I believe is the meaning of all nature, the development of varied forms of free and beautiful experience.

In what way does freedom of the sense of beauty in us surpass that in birds? Of our six standards of song, it is the second, or scope—complexity and variety—in which birds are chiefly deficient, in comparison with ourselves. A bird's repertoire is a matter of one or two, or a half-dozen, or at most fifty or a hundred, little patterns; and the larger the number, the simpler the patters are likely to be. A bird's repertoire could be scored musically with a few, or at the most a few hundred notes; a human musician's, only with millions of notes. This is but the beginning of the difference in complexity. And only the simpler bird songs have the degree of unity of a human composition.

As to freedom, human beings can symbolize innumerable diverse patterns of thought, feeling and action, and insofar as they are free, they can select among these patterns. The patterns can occupy any length of time from seconds to years. A bird grasps definite patterns occupying a few seconds, never minutes, not to mention days or years.

The longest quite definite song pattern which any bird has been shown to have memorized or recognized is much less than half a minute. Longer patterns are not repeated in a definite way, but are random combinations of short patterns.

Human superiority is in the complexity of the patterns we can apprehend, and the lengths of time they stretch over. This enables us to recognize and memorize not only words and brief sentences, as a parrot can, but long sentences, paragraphs, and essays; it enables us to follow grammatical relationships whose clear exhibition requires memory beyond a few seconds; or we can follow chains of inference which likewise require a long memory span. Our whole symbolic and rational power depends upon a grasp of complex patterns organizing stretches of time utterly beyond the grasp of other animals. Our freedom is between elaborate systems of patterns not just little bits of pattern; between whole designs for living, not just little actions here and now.

Let us next consider the question of individuality as treated by science. In dealing with this question, I find myself unable to resist the temptation to deal with some rather grim topics. They are grim partly because of the inadequacies of habits formed in our prescientific past. Perhaps I shall also give myself away as an ex-Yankee. The simplest systems in nature, such as atoms, or one-celled plants and animals, are those in which there is least room for individual variations. The most complex systems, the higher animals, are those in which individuality can be and is at its maximum. If the essential human power is the symbolic power on a complex level, due to the ability to follow patterns through long time stretches, together with some freedom of selection with respect to these patterns, then it is obvious that, with respect to such power and freedom, there will be scope for individual differences which utterly dwarf any such differences in the lower animals. Perhaps one dog can in a fashion understand a few words or phrases, and another dog not any; but one human being may understand or invent a million phrases, and another, if he or she is an idiot, none at all. Each of the million phrases may be in a language unintelligible to most other human individuals on earth.But even within a single language, the different things which may be said are beyond counting. Compared to individual differences of this kind, certain classifications of people are trivial in the extreme. It is absolutely sure, and this is one of the rockbottom facts of human life, that in comparison with the almost infinite individual differences in symbols behavior, that is, in specifically human behavior, any differences between men as such and women as such, or one racial group and other, or between groups which science can now define by merely physical characteristics, such as geographical origin of their ancestors, are as one to a billion.. A born idiot, or a person in a catatonic state, no matter of what sex or race, can no more compose music, or use language to communicate. than a bird, indeed less so. There are all degrees of such deficiencies; and practically all of them, so far as we know, may occur in any physically delimited group of human endeavor.

I must confess I often wonder how many persons there still are wherever you please, who have never lived for a thoughtful quarter of an hour with this basic fact that the big human differences are individual, not racial.

To say that, "all are born equal" is unfortunately more likely to confuse than to clarify this matter. I believe Jefferson's phrase can be defended; but it is at best almost sure to mislead. We are not all born equal in any important sense whatever, except that we are all helpless at first, and die at last; and our inequalities are vastly important. Jefferson, of course, knew this; but one of the things he had in mind was this: The only reliable way to ascertain individual differences in capacity is to give everyone the chance to see what he or she can do. What women will do will be known only in so far as they are permitted and encouraged to try to do whatever they can. And so with other physically defined groups.

One mockingbird is nearly as good as another. The human species is that animal species in which vast individual contrasts are the rule. With a thousand words, millions of billions of sentences can be made; and so every one of us, I suppose, says things each day no one has ever said before. These sentences are not mere sequences; they express unitary ideas. In this way we all add to the variety, the scope, of the cosmic beauty. To lump together low-garde morons and geniuses, the hopelessly insane and those in sound mental health, doctors, lawyers and ditchdiggers, criminals and saintly persons, and then contrast, as racists do, such an almost meaningless group of incomparable individuals with another of equally heterogeneous ones, and to argue about the relative merits of rights of the two group, is to emphasize the trivial at the expense of the important. The vast inequality of individuals, in terms of their behavioral capacities, makes any other intrinsic inequality almost negligible. Even birds are unique individuals, as careful observers learn; but incomparably more so are human beings. Each one makes a more or less free and distinctive contribution to the beauty of the world; but where the great contributions are to come from, no one can ell. And it is the individual, or spiritually united group, which contributes, which composes or performs music, speaks bravely, kindly, timorously, or harshly, is slow- of quick-witted. It is not all people as such, or all women as such, or all pink persons as such.

Nature is a vast system productive of the enjoyment of beauty and freedom. We are in a radical sense the freest of the creatures on this planet. We are for that reason capable both of the greatest achievements and of the greatest mistakes. We can achieve the richest patterns; we also can destroy patterns; we can enjoy rich harmonies, and also torture or annihilate ourselves and other animals. More and more our very existence depends upon our learning to cherish and judge real individual capacities. If we want a canary to listen to, we need not care too much which individual canary it is, since most of them sing well, and none very much better than the majority. But if a person wants a friend, or a parent a teacher of children, he or she had better care which particular woman and man it is, for there are vast differences. If we choose our friends, teachers, and acquaintances by a crude physical criterion, then in that way and to that extent we are exhibiting insensitivity to enormous spiritual distinctions. We are in effect, to put it bluntly, materialists. And if we distribute opportunities by similarly crude or irrelevant physical criteria, then we are treating as comparatively negligible differences in capacity which in fact are gigantic.

Whereas songbirds are evaluated chiefly by species, sometimes by geographical races, in short by physically bounded groups, human beings deserve to be evaluated chiefly as individuals, for they are behavioristically a quintillionfold more highly individualized than any other animal group. They are also incomparably more free. This individuality and freedom are the glory of humanity; we have no other. Our glory is not our color or shape but our artistic and creative power, the immeasurable uniqueness of our every experience and act, in a world in which habit and instinct leave open only tiny details for the creative choices of the lower animals.

There is one final question: For what or whom is the beauty of the world? Birds were singing ages before there were human beings to hear them. Even now the vast majority of songs fall upon no human ears. True, birds themselves enjoy the songs, if my arguments are sound. But this only means that their experiences, while they last, have some internal harmony and intensity of feeling. But they do not last. Neither do ours. For what or whom, after we and the birds are gone, will it all have been? For nothing? Then life is a tale told by an idiot, signifying nothing. One can say these words, but one cannot express them in one's life. Life which goes on at all cannot be denying its own value in such wholesale fashion.

A favorite answer is, personal immortality. But then what about the birds. Will they have lived for nothing? Also, personal immortality is forever beyond our possible knowledge. Even could we know that individuals had survived death, we still should not and could not know that they will survive forever. Some say the answer is posterity, but, once more, what about the birds? And further, what is to prove that any one of us in the infinitude of the long run will have contributed to posterity; even if-- which we could not possibly know-- the human race itself will forever escape destruction?

There is one plain answer to the question: What is the world's beauty for? It is for the sole conceivable mind which could possibly appreciate that beauty as a whole and in all its aspects, the cosmic or divine mind. Moreover, while we could not know ourselves or the species to be immortal, we might be able to know that God was so. We only need to know that God exists, as the supreme guiding influence in all things, upon whom all else depends for existence. I believe we can know that there is such a guiding power. How else, for one thing, can the multitude of beings, each with its own freedom, form an ordered system? Darwinism explains brilliantly how higher forms of life proceed from lower, but it is presupposed that the basic order of the world is maintained. An order from which so much harmonious freedom can spring is as providential as anything the older teleology could give us. And on the old view, monstrosities and suffering had to be explained. If we take freedom seriously, realizing that causal laws are merely the statistical limits within which freedom operates, we can then see that the role of providence is not to rule out chance or danger from existence but to see to it that the chances for evil are justified by the chances for good. Risks are compensated for by opportunities; both have the same origin, the limited freedom of the creatures. Providence is the limiting or guidance of freedom s that the inevitable risks are not unduly great. That Darwinism makes chance fundamental means that it makes the freedom of the creatures efficacious. <u>They</u> decide the details of their lives, and collectively they even decide the course of evolution itself in the long run. As Kingsley, an English clergyman, put it in a novel, nature "makes things make themselves" and, we may add, makes them also make their descendants. I fail to see that the old teleology was half as satisfying as this. By supposing God to determine everything, it made all distinctions between good and evil nonessential. If God determines everything, then "whatever is is right," which means that nothing in any intelligible sense is right.

Our ancestors had a phrase which, though they scarcely seemed to know what they meant by it, can still be used to express the answer I have given to the question, For whom is the beauty of the world? They said, The world exists for the glory of God. I take this to mean, it exists for God to cherish in all its aspects of accumulating variety and harmony. By our creative freedom we contribute unique values to the all-embracing life, the ever-growing treasure of imperishable values. The privilege of making these contributions will seem insufficient, I suspect, only to those who have never learned to appreciate the beauty which surrounds us, the capacities for creation of beauty which are within us, and the sublime beauty of the idea of consciousness for whom the least individual in creation has its own unique flavor and interest.

Charles Hartshorne

CAN WE PROVE THE
EXISTENCE OF GOD?

This is an essay in "natural theology," that is to say, theology through the reason which is inherent in man's nature and without benefit of grace or "special" revelation. It is a doctrine of the Roman Catholic Church that natural theology is possible and that without this possibility, revelation would lose its reasonableness. Although I am not a Romanist, I honor the theologians who have steadily maintained this tenet through the centuries of discredit into which natural theology has passed since Hume and Kant. However, we do live in a different age, and if we are to find a basis in reason for religion it cannot be in so simple a way as that of the great founders of the metaphysics of religion.

My first suggestion is that although natural theology does not argue from revealed premises, it may quite properly allow revelation to suggest what the topic for consideration is to be. It may allow revealed religion, or what claims to be such, to furnish the question, even though not the answer. Here I am apparently saying the opposite of what Tillich says. I am saying that revelation defines the question, while philosophy, or secular reason, gives the answer. If the task is to form a rational theory about the central religious idea, the idea of God, it seems proper to begin by asking religion, including revealed religion, what it means by "God." For if natural theology is not to support belief in the God who is worshipped, why speak of "theology" at all? "Theos" is basically a religious word.

If God is the one who is worshipped, what is worship? Tillich profoundly argues that the Great Commandment to love God with all one's being amounts to a definition at once of worship and of the term God. Whatever can be loved in integral fashion, that is, can be worshipped, is God. I take this to be the proper way to use the term. Any description of God incompatible with this requirement is a misuse of words, a changing of the subject. I believe that Spinoza's description of his deity was in some features incompatible with his claim to worship that deity.

In my opinion the great theologians as well as philosophers of our tradition were primarily (in one way or another) guilty unconsciously of changing the subject and misusing the word God. They identified deity with the wholly absolute, infinite, or eternal. But worship as such does not imply this, and indeed, I hold, is incompatible with it. No one can love the mere absolute with all his being. He cannot even love it with all his intellectual being; for intellect is concerned with the relative and the changing, as well as with the absolute or immutable. In Augustine's essay on Free Will one sees clearly the strange notion that the mathematician as such is peculiarly close to God, which implies that the historian, or anyone concerned with historical processes, must be very far from Him. Numbers, for Augustine, are close to God because they are immutable; it follows that people, who are highly changeable, must be far from God. This may be rather typical Greek philosophy, but what has it to do with Jewish or Christian or Islamic religion? No one today thinks that the mathematician, as compared, say, to the theoretical physicist, is peculiarly godlike. And what about the poor historian? Is he looking straight away from deity?

We are no longer Greeks in philosophy. We realize that immutability may only mean utter abstractness. Numbers are immutable because they are so little, not because they are so much. In their concrete use, to explain actual processes, numbers are invaluable instruments, but merely in themselves they are only superb intellectual toys, and it is not in their direction primarily that we must seek the greatest of all realities.

Omniscience and omnipotence, viewed through Greek spectacles as wholly immutable, generate antinomies, which some take as occasions for awe and intellectual humility. But humility and awe are not the same as love, and cannot alone fulfill the great commandment. The tortures which religious people have long endured through trying to reconcile purely eternal knowledge, or the omnipotence of a wholly absolute being, with the freedom of our temporal acts, or with the occurrence of suffering and other forms of evil, have often been downright masochistic. And I do not think they have a proper place in genuine love of God.

How then is God to be described, beyond saying thatGod is worthy of being worshipped? On the one hand, if there are limits to God's perfection, or if dependent upon others for worth, God cannot, it seems, merit worship. Can "unconditional" devotion have a "conditioned" terminus or ground? asks Tillich. So he infers the unconditionedness of God from the definition of worship. But this is either an extremely vague or ambiguous use of words, or else it is just the old Greek error against which I, and not only I, have long been protesting. For whether one says "absolute" or "unconditioned" is of no consequence, since the clear meaning, if any, is the same. And "immutable" is implied in either case. Is our love for God immutable? Moreover, no one interested, as we are bound to be, in history, in change, can possibly love the immutable with all of his or her being. Only by self-deception can we suppose ourselves to do this.

Yet, on the other hand, if one gives up terms like absolute, infinite, or immutable altogether in describing God, does that not also conflict with worship? Can we, without reservation, devote ourselves to serving One whose knowledge or goodness is limited, or in whom everything is subject to alteration? The church fathers, the classical theologians generally, had excellent reasons for supposing that absoluteness, infinity, and eternity must somehow apply to the divine. What they failed to see was that relativity, finitude, and change, for equally good reasons, must also apply and that the task of reason in theology is to reconcile the two sets of requirements, not to give monopolistic privileges to one or the other. I have shown, in various writings (for instance, in The Divine Relativity), that this reconciliation is possible or, at least, that no obvious contradiction results. And the claim has not, so far, been refuted.

We now come to the key question of natural theology: taking God to have both infinity and finitude, both absoluteness and relativity, both eternity and alterability, each in just the fashion required by the definition of worship, what can reason say as to the reality of the deity thus defined? Here we face an old topic, the theistic proofs. Hume,

Kant, and others are supposed to have demolished these, once for all. And theologians have sometimes said good riddance. There are, however, some flaws in this conception of intellectual history.

First Hume and, even more, Kant were imprisoned in the Greek bias which tended to identify eternity, infinity, absoluteness, with divinity. This presupposition plays a decisive role in their conception of the proofs. And indeed, the objection to the identification of God with the absolute is not only that it changes the subject from the God of worship to something else (really a philosophical idol), but also that the notion of a purely absolute, infinite, and eternal reality is riddled with antinomies, if taken as anything but an abstraction wholly incapable of existing save as an element in something more concrete. Any alleged proof for so illogical a conclusion must be equally illogical. Therefore, the failure of the classical proofs as they stand is indeed good riddance. But only because they were proofs, not for God, but for an idolatrous absurdity.

Second, Hume and Kant argued against natural theology from premises which not only begged the question, but are today highly controversial. The Newtonian world picture was implicitly antitheistic, and to argue from it was to prejudge the theological issue. Accordingly, the collapse of this world picture reopens and recasts the fundamental questions of natural theology. Many philosophers heap scorn upon theologians who find evidences for God in quantum mechanics. But they are missing the main point, which is that Newtonian physics, taken literally, as it was usually, though wrongly, taken, implies the unreality of God. A cosmic engineer is not God; it cannot be loved with all one's being, not even if the engineer is said to make the material with which he or she works. A world-machine, a pseudoconcept at best, could not be a divine creation. The view of the world as essentially machine-like was, to be sure, no result of scientific inquiry, but an unlimited extrapolation such as only philosophy could possibly justify. And no philosophy could justify it either, for it was an internally incoherent doctrine, as Peirce, Bergson, Whitehead, and others have shown. We may well rejoice that we are rid of this incubus. But the consequences for religious metaphysics have yet to be widely appreciated. Cultural lag is greater in philosophy than in any other subject, even though in no subject, perhaps, is there so much anticipation of cultural developments.

A third weakness of Hume's and Kant's alleged refutation of the possibility of theistic proofs is the lack of an adequate understanding, such as is possible today, of what it means to try to "prove" a philosophical doctrine. Hume and Kant themselves offer proofs for various philosophical contentions of their own; however, like all proofs outside of formal logic, finite arithmetic, and pure geometry, these Humian and Kantian proofs rely upon premises which are open to controversy. And indeed, if the alleged impossibility of theistic proofs only means that any such proof must have more or less controversial premises, then theism may be in no worse case than any other philosophical view. To draw the conclusion that the divine existence is a mere matter of faith is to imply that the whole of philosophy is a mere matter of faith. And this is scarcely what Hume and Kant intended. Some contemporary philosophers who reject natural theology may perhaps be willing to accept such a radical conclusion. Thus Wittgenstein says that philosophizing, as he practices it, makes no assertions—and, I suppose, no denials. Even so, would he want to say that theoretical reason is in no sense operative in philosophy?

In view of the three weaknesses listed above, I maintain that Hume and Kant proved nothing for or against the possibility of rational grounds for theistic belief. (1) They changed the subject from the God of religion to a philosophical idol of absoluteness; (2) they reasoned from question-begging and, as we can see today, highly dubious premises; and (3) they had an inadequate grasp of what can be meant by rational argument in philosophy. Have contemporary philosophical critics of natural theology overcome these defects? I am not aware that they have. Mostly they rely upon Hume and Kant, with casual emendations, elaborations, or extensions.

But perhaps contemporary theological critics of the claims of natural theology to prove the existence of God have shown their illegitimacy? I cannot see this either. It is not enough to appeal to the fall of man and the corruption of human reason. Such ideas are too vague to be decisive, even if one grants that from the standpoint of a certain revelation they are to be accepted. Theologians too are under the fall, even when they reason about natural theology, or anything else. Appeal to such a blanket defect can hardly illuminate definite issues very much.

Schweitzer and also Brunner argue that theoretical reason is bound to go astray when confronting nature and human life, with their mixtures of good and evil, of realized ideals and frustrations. Must not the dilemma always arise: either explain away the evils by a false idealization of reality or deny the perfection of divine power and goodness? However, the answer is that, in fact we have had philosophers who have done neither of these things. Nor is there any logical necessity for doing either. If "perfection" is used in the religiously appropriate sense, God's perfect power and goodness need not imply that the evils in the world must be God's doing. There is, therefore, no forced option between denying divine power or goodness and denying the reality of evil. In short, this argument against the power of reason to deal with religious questions is fallacious. It is an illicit generalization from an oversimplified view of the history of philosophy and of the logic of certain concepts.

It is time we came to grips with the question of proofs, that is, rational grounds for belief. In a formal proof a set of premises, which we may put into a single complex premise p, logically entails a conclusion q. So we reason "p, therefore q." To this it is always possible to reply, "I do not accept p, hence—so far as the argument goes—I need not accept q." The old-fashioned idea, however, was that in some cases this way out is impossible, since p is in those cases self-evident and undeniable. But through the centuries we have learned the hard way that strictly undeniable premises are scarce, particularly undeniable premises having controversial conclusions. In this sense, it may well be impossible to prove the existence of God, if "proof" means valid reasoning from premises that only an utter blockhead or dishonest person could deny. But then would not every philosophically interesting doctrine also turn out to be unprovable? And if this means that there is no scope for reason in the subject perhaps we philosophers should have the grace to stop pretending and go out of business!

The value of a formal proof is not that it establishes its conclusion for everyone, no matter what her or his assumptions and attitudes, but that it establishes a logical price for rejecting a certain conclusion. If the conclusion does follow from the premise, the minimal logical price of rejecting the conclusion is rejecting the premise. Of those who question the conclusion, some will already be aware of this price, and be willing to pay it; some will not be aware of it but, upon learning that it is the price, will find themselves just as able to reject the premise as the conclusion; but finally, some who have not previously understood the price of unbelief will feel this price to be so high that they will want to reconsider the matter. And then suppose that they can be shown that still other premises entail the conclusion, and suppose they find the rejection of these other premises likewise difficult, so that the logical price of unbelief comes to appear to them far higher than they at first suspected—can anyone deny that this might suffice to turn unbelief into belief?

If a valid proof is thus one which, for some persons at least, makes the logical price of unbelief appear unbearably high, then I am confident that there can be theistic proofs. And I hold that they can be of great importance, so that, on this issue, the Roman Catholic Church is to be congratulated on its steadiness and courage. I take the theistic proofs, properly stated and fairly evaluated, to be as intellectually respectable as philosophical arguments are likely to be, and I am not yet ready to admit that this is not saying anything. I also think, however, that the traditional statements, and traditional evaluations, of the proofs are mostly careless, sloppy, or unfair. In no portion of their responsibility, perhaps, have members of my profession done so poorly as in this one. Historical reasons for this cannot be gone into here. Some of them have already been hinted at.

The time has come for some examples of theistic proof. The logical price of denying the reality of God can be exhibited in various ways, each of which can be put in the form of a dilemma, or better still, a trilemma. For instance, if theism is defended by saying: the world is orderly, order implies an orderer, the only conceivable orderer for a world is God, then the unbeliever is by implication doing one or more of the following: denying that there is order in the world, denying that order implies an orderer, or denying that the power to order a world implies divinity. Of course there are those who are ready to make one or more of these denials. But the three propositions in question can be so presented as to make their denial seem counter-intuitive to some of us. For us, the argument is a valid one. This is all that any philosophical argument accomplishes, when you "get right down to it."

Let us outline the argument in more detail. (1) A simply unordered world is a contradiction in terms; it is no object of possible knowledge and there is no way to distinguish it clearly from nothing at all, (2) order among existing individuals means some unitary influence or power acting upon those individuals; finally, (3) only power superior in principle to ordinary powers, only divine power, could constitute the cosmic orderer.

It is irrelevant to point out that there is disorder in the world as well as order. For, in the first place, we are not asking how can there be perfect cosmic order, but only how can there be anything but cosmic chaos, anything but unthinkable confusion. And in the second place, to say that order consists in a superior power influencing all other powers is not only different from saying that the superior power is the only power, a sheer monopoly; it is even incompatible with saying this. "Omnipotence" as a pure monopoly of power or decision-making is a pseudo-concept, and has nothing to do with the argument we are discussing. And only this pseudo-concept implies that the worldorder must or could be absolute, free from any elements of disorder or partial chaos. As Hume and Kant failed to see, the supreme power cannot be the sole power, for then "supreme" would have no meaning. Also, if there is a multiplicity of powers, and if a "power" which fails to influence any effect is meaningless, then the total cosmic effect cannot be determined by the supreme power alone. Even supreme power can only impose limits on the disagreements, conflicts, or confusions among lesser powers; it cannot simply eliminate these confusions, for this would require its becoming the sole power, and this is nonsense. Power acts upon power, not upon the powerless. Activity and passivity belong together; what cannot act cannot be acted upon, and what cannot be acted upon cannot act. Both God and the creatures must influence reality as a whole, and there must be mutual influence between God and creatures. I cannot here further defend these principles.

We must move on. Why not, some would say, suppose that there can be order even without an ordering power? This would mean that a multitude of individuals, by blind chance, necessity, or deliberate intention, cooperated to produce or maintain a world order. Cooperation does occur, for instance, in the work of a committee. But the first act of cooperation is to choose a chairman, if one has not already been provided in the act of setting up the committee. Also the committee must have been given a directive from someone, if it is to know what its cooperation is to be about. In politics, which is the high-level obvious case best known in our experience, it is the "rule of one" which alone enables chaos to be avoided. If there is not a ruler, one must be created, even though that rule is narrowly limited in time, function, or both, and though the person may be called chairman or president, not ruler. But the ability to cooperate enough to choose a ruler presupposes a more basic order, and this order must be traced back either to previous acts of influential individuals persuading the rest into a decent degree of conformity, or to "laws of nature." Now the laws of nature are the very question at issue, not an explanation. Political laws we understand, we know how they originate and in what they consist; but how there can be laws of nature is the riddle we seek to unravel. The political analogy has not been shown to be irrelevant or absurd, provided it is properly formulated. The ultimate principles are: (a) order is explained by the influence of one upon many; (b) this influence in turn implies some sort of superiority of the one to the many; and (c) the possibility of universal or cosmic ordering implies a universal superiority such as is clearly conceivable only through the idea of divinity.

I believe that the foregoing outline could be strengthened by developing various lines of collateral reasoning. But I wish instead to present another theistic proof. This is the ethical proof. In ethics we need to assume that, taking their consequences into account, some modes of action are better than others. For if right ways of acting do not, in general at least, produce better consequences than wrong ways, what is the point of right and wrong? But consequences may be divided into immediate or short run and more or less remote or long run. Both are in principle relevant. If it were the case that doing good to my neighbor now must result in his or her greater misery later on, or if doing good to my children must result to a greater extent in misery for my grandchildren, how in either case could I feel obligated to do the more immediate good? But on the other hand, how much do we know about the long-run effects of our acts? We and every subsequent generation will presumably die in the end; and the human race itself will eventually perish, or at least will change beyond any knowable limit, and beyond any definitely traceable benefit from our individual actions. How, in all this, can we understand a long-run outcome of our nobler and wiser actions which will be definitely better than the long-run outcome of our most unkind, cowardly, or foolish ones? In the grave, what will it matter? Or, is it the fate of posterity through an infinity of millennia which we should be concerned with? since we cannot possibly have any definite knowledge, or even imagining, of such an infinity of human survival, our basic ethical notion of ultimate consequences seems to vanish into total indefiniteness.

Here then is the argument. Admitted that the aim of life is the service of God, and that the long-run good we accomplish is our contribution to the divine "glory" (in the old and perhaps unnecessarily mysterious language), then neither our own death nor the ultimate fate of humanity can prevent us from having done better by acting nobly and wisely than by acting ignobly and foolishly. For it is not perishable generations we are seeking ultimately to serve but imperishable deity; it is not a forgetful and perhaps foolish posterity, or a humanity after immeasurable changes, on this changing planet or elsewhere, that we hope finally to benefit, but a divine life definitely able to cherish with adequate wisdom each transient beauty of human experience in everlasting remembrance. Deny such a divine cherishing and remembrance and what becomes of the idea that right actions have better consequences than wrong ones? The unbeliever faces a trilemma: (1) the short-run human consequences; or (2) the long-run consequences for the human race (or all sentient creatures); or (3) the long-run consequences for individuals conceived as surviving death forever. One or more of these must constitute the ultimate value of our behavior. The first proposal (short-run consequences only) seems to destroy any genuine rationality in ethics; the second and the third (the immortality of the species or the individual) must remain wholly indeterminate for human knowledge. This is a part of the price of non-belief, that there can be no positive rational aim, intelligible as such. The service of God, on the contrary, is positive, rational, and, for the believer, intelligible. For the unbeliever, there can only be a vague hope that somehow something good, we know not what, will in the long run ensue from our efforts.

This argument, too, has been poorly presented in the literature;

indeed, it is so little known as to have scarcely been evaluated at all, even unfairly. Usually the contribution to ethics accredited to belief has been in the form of "sanctions," heavenly rewards and hellish punishments, a lamentable business of contradictorily asking us to act from love of others and of God, while yet telling us that unless it is possible to act rightly from desire of self-advantage or fear of self-disadvantage, we cannot be expected to act rightly at all. Sanctions can only be needed for the unethical, but then at most hell alone, and not heaven, could be relevant! This way of arguing for God I wholly repudiate.

God is needed, not so that there can be human advantage in the ultimate long run for good acts and human disadvantage in the long run for bad acts, but so that the ultimate human long run need not concern us at all, but only the human present and relative long run (which alone we have any power to know). Our need is not for an ultimate aim of self-advantage, or human advantage, but for an ultimate aim—period. If people can sometimes do things out of love for children or posterity rather than concern for their own futures, then still more can they do things for God, who alone is wholly lovable, and whose future alone is secure from death and corrupting change. To suppose that in doing things for God we must be motivated finally by concern for our human futures is to imply that God is less lovable even than human beings! This only brings into the open how little some people have understood what worship of God is all about.

Besides the fixation on sanctions, the other chief reason why the proof from the necessity for a rational aim has been largely overlooked is the fixation on "the absolute" (or "unconditioned") as the very definition of deity. Of course one cannot bestow benefits upon "the absolute," the wholly immutable or infinite. So much the worse for this definition of God, which makes "serving" him at best a deceptive disguise for the creatures' service of themselves and one another. A "glory of God" which it can be our aim to promote cannot be simply absolute; for the merely absolute or unconditioned is not possibly promoted, enriched, enhanced, furthered—in plain English, it is not served in any reasonable sense whatever.

It should scarcely need saying that every legitimate aim which an unbeliever can have, such as promoting human happiness, is included in the aim of serving God. For what benefit can we bestow upon the divine except by realizing in our life, and favoring in the lives of other creatures, the actualization of such values as our—and their—inborn constitutions make possible? As Hume said so well, there is nothing of value we could possibly offer God except human (or creaturely) happiness. If our humility or "obedience" serves God, it can only be because it is required for creaturely happiness or welfare. To say otherwise is to put God on the level of tyrants, basically insecure rulers, who need to be reassured as to the status of their preeminence. The "good life for man or other creatures" is then also man's only gift to God. But all of it is such a gift. Hence the humanistic objectives are entirely embraced in theistic religion.

I have outlined two arguments illustrating the logical price of unbelief. There are at least four others of comparable power. There is an argument from truth, or from the idea of knowledge, which I call the epistemic or idealistic argument—the latter because it is chiefly idealists who have developed it, especially Josiah Royce, though they failed, I think, to put it into a wholly correct form. There is an aesthetic argument, from the idea of beauty or harmony of experience as implying harmony in the inclusive object of experience. There is the cosmological argument from the contingency of the world, which Hume and Kant mis-stated and, in my opinion, did not really refute. There is finally the ontological argument invented, but not adequately analyzed, by Anselm, and essentially misunderstood by all of its famous critics, as I claim to have shown in two books. The ontological argument confronts us with a trilemma: (1) The idea of God lacks consistent cognitive meaning (the positivistic position); (2) The idea of God has consistent meaning, and what it describes exists, but only in fact, not by any a priori necessity; (3) The idea of God has consistent meaning, but what it describes in fact fails to exist.

1. The greatest difficulty confronting the Anselmian is to disprove the first or positivistic horn of the trilemma. Here Anselm was weakest, though it is just here that critics generally fail to attack him. But notice that if positivism is correct, then theism could not be true, for a question can have an answer only if the question makes sense. Kant failed to see that if he really refuted the argument, he also refuted theism itself.

2. That God exists in mere fact, not by a priori necessity, would indeed mean that the ontological inference is fallacious. For only what is a priori can be formally proved. But Anselm really did show, as I have argued in many writings, that to exist contingently, or so that non-existence would have been possible, is to exist as other than divine. Only that which could not conceivably fail to exist can be unsurpassable or worthy of worship, and only that which is unsurpassable could not conceivably fail to exist.

3. If God could not exist contingently, or in mere fact, he also could not contingently fail to exist. The question, then, is not an empirical one at all, but in the broad sense logical, a question of meaning. The non-existence of unsurpassability can only mean its inconceivability. Against this positivistic alternative one can object: (a) If there is a contradiction, let it be pointed out. (b) The capacity of the idea of God to explicate the meaning of cosmic order, the meaning of a rational aim in ethics, and to solve other categorical problems, seems incompatible with its being without cognitive import. In this way the other theistic proofs strengthen the ontological at its weakest point, the assumption of consistent meaning. At the same time, and without vicious circularity, the ontological proof can strengthen the other proofs at their weakest points. For, these proofs start with categories which seem required to deal with basic human problems, and so their meaning and consistency can reasonably be assumed, but without the ontological proof one might look upon theism as merely one among competing explanations of basic features of reality. The ontological proof, however, shows that there can be no competing explanations, since if the theistic explanation is genuinely conceivable it must be uniquely true. Thus this proof shows that no issue of empirical fact can be involved, but only necessities of meaning. If theism is logically tenable, it is true; if it is not true, then it is somehow illogical and could not be true, no matter what may or may not be observed in any experience.

I believe, however, that any of the proofs, adequately developed, will by itself give good support to the same conclusion as the others, and that the premises of all the proofs would be intuitively convincing if we could think clearly enough. Weak and strong points in the proofs are ultimately subjective or psychological matters. Even the distinction between the proofs is due to lack of clarity in our thinking. Either theism is rational and necessarily true, and all competing theories irrational and necessarily false, or theism is irrational and could not be true. Proofs are but ways of trying to exhibit the unique rationality of theism as a metaphysical doctrine. And in my judgment the greater burden of proof is in any case not upon theism. The fruitful attitude in all knowledge is not to ask for proof, but to ask for disproof. Popper's emphasis upon falsification is to the point. When Kant said that God could neither be proved nor disproved, he ought to have asked himself, what can it mean to say that a doctrine, against which there could be no evidence, yet might be false? If we could not know the non-existence of God, who could? Obviously God Himself could not know his own non-existence. And if this non-existence could not be known by anyone, is it not a meaningless notion? But then either theism is necessarily true or positivism is so, and in the latter case, there is no room for faith. Faith is senseless unless truth is at least possible. I hold that the divine non-existence is not a logically legitimate notion and that everyone who is unwilling to espouse the positivistic denial of meaning to theism ought to accept its truth.

The believer need only be sure of one thing, that one's belief is not absurd. And if it is absurd, then so, it seems, is the idea of rational ethics, or of a value to human life from the standpoint of the ultimate long run. And then what is not absurd? The existentialists unwittingly support the theistic argument by terming life itself an absurdity. For in that case, any belief is as good as any other, for belief expresses life and cannot do anything else. I find it incomparably more reasonable to suppose that life and belief in the cosmic harmonizer of life and summator of its achievements are alike free from essential absurdity.

Charles Hartshorne

THE DEVELOPMENT OF
PROCESS PHILOSOPHY

The term, "process philosophy" is one way of pointing to a profound change which has come over speculative philosophy or metaphysics in the modern period in Europe and America. I have myself often used the more noncommittal phrase "neoclassical metaphysics" for much the same purpose, since the emphasis upon process or becoming, though essential, is only one feature of this new way of viewing reality. Also characteristic is the emphasis upon relations and relativity. The Buddhistic phrase, "dependent origination," suggests the connection between the two points. What has an origin is relative to that origin; only what has always been as it is can be "absolute," wholly independent of other things. In this essay I shall deal chiefly with process, not relativity. It is not hard to translate talk about being and becoming into talk about absoluteness and relativity, but I shall not always attempt the translation in what follows.

Greek philosophy tended to depreciate becoming and exalt mere being, and—as was consistent—to depreciate relativity and exalt independence or absoluteness. Aristotle summed it up when he held that what was altogether immutable and hence immune to influence from others was superior to that which in any way changed or depended upon other things. Medieval natural theology never explicitly deviated from this attitude, though revealed doctrines of the trinity and the incarnation may have almost explicitly done so (Did not the Son depend upon the Father without being inferior to Him?).

However, the harmony of some doctrines of the classical natural theology with the Greek attitude is extremely doubtful. Aristotle had denied God's knowledge of contingent and changing things, on the

111

straightforward ground that knowing cannot be independent of what is known. Yet Christian and most Jewish and Mohammedan theists felt obliged, for religious reasons, to affirm God's knowledge of the contingent and changing world. Only a few Mohammedans dared even to hint that this must mean change in God. Christians and Jews would scarcely go so far. The result was a glaring inconsistency which troubled many. For precisely this reason Crescas, and later Spinoza, denied contingency (and by implication change) not only in God but in the world which God knows, for they saw that the known is in the knowing, and if there is contingency and change in the former then there is also in the latter. Thus in Spinoza, the Greek bias came to its last great triumph in Western thought. Not only God, but the world, too, was to be made safe from accident or genuine alteration, and indeed, immutable omniscience, implying the immutability of all truth, consorts ill with the view that becoming is real. If there is novel reality, then to that extent the truth also must be novel. To say of future events that they "are going to be" is to imply that their entire character is a present fact, though a fact which, with our human limitations, we have not yet reached, but there the fact is, waiting for us to reach it, or there it is offstage, waiting to come on. In this view, genuine becoming is missing. The truth, the reality, is eternally there, spread out to the divine gaze, though our present experience, being localized in the eternal panorama, cannot behold most of it. As St. Thomas put it, events in time are like travelers on a road who cannot see those far ahead of them though they can all be seen by one sufficiently high above the road looking down upon its entire length, i.e., by God in eternity. Bergson's phrase, "spatializing time," fits this view as a glove a hand. The theory entirely omits the aspect of creation involved in becoming. The entirety of creation cannot be viewed if there is no such totality. How can there be if the actual sum of events receives additions each moment? What is becoming if not such perpetual adding of new realities? Thomas is assuming the falsity of a certain view of time; process philosophy adopts this view, and not without reason.

Since the eternalistic view reached explicit formulation in theological guise, it was fitting that the process doctrine should also emerge in a theological context. Philosophies of being, which treat becoming as secondary, have acquired powerful religious sanctions; it is therefore well that we should realize from the outset that process philosophy, in its origin at least, is a rival religious doctrine rather than an irreligious one. This is true in two important respects. First, the earliest great tradition which espoused a philosophy of becoming was Buddhism. Heraclitus, who said that things are new each moment, was isolated, and in addition obscure, for we have but fragmentary sayings. Only the followers of Buddha produced a great literature expressive of the doctrine that becoming is the universal form of reality. They carried this view through, in some respects, with admirable thoroughness, long before anything like it occurred in the West. Philosophies of being characteristically treat change either as "unreal" or as in principle but the substitution of one set of qualities for another in an abiding "substratum," "substance," or "subject of change." For them, reality consists essentially of beings, not happenings or events. If a being is not of the highest kind, it shows this deficiency by undergoing alterations. If it is of the highest kind, alteration could only be for the worse and hence could have no point. So the highest being is changeless, but the others, poor things, keep changing, apparently in the, in principle, vain effort to make up for their imperfection. This doctrine is Greek through and through, but, alas, the Church Fathers accepted it. True, the doctrine also arose long ago in the Orient, but there Buddhism came to challenge it, with a subtlety and persistence which had no counterpart in classical and medieval Europe. The Buddhists rejected "substance," including the "soul" as substance. The momentary experiences are the primary realities, and these do not change, they simply become, and what is called change is the successive becoming of events having certain relationships to their predecessors. The "soul" or the self-identical ego is merely the relatedness of experiences to their predecessors through memory and the persistence of various qualities or personality traits. The first great metaphysician in the West to hold this view clearly was Whitehead, in the present century. But we must not get ahead of our story, which is mainly that of the development of process philosophy in the West.

Secondly, the man who first squarely faced the conflict between the religious doctrine of an all-knowing God and Greek eternalism, and decided against the latter, was Fausto Socinus, whose sect was destroyed by persecution and whose bold theorizing has been ignored by historians of philosophy—not to their credit, I must add. Socinus rejected the immutability of God in order to be able consistently to affirm the reality of becoming. He did not quite put it in this way. What he said was that human freedom is incompatible with immutable divine knowledge of our free acts. Our freedom is nothing but that case of becoming which we experience from the inside or by direct intuition, rather than infer from more or less indirect observation. We have to start with events we intimately know. A decision—and we make little ones each moment—is a settling of the otherwise unsettled; it occurs in time, not in eternity. To say that God eternally knows all decisions is to imply that the totality of decisions is a single, all-inclusive eternally complete set of realities, but then there is nothing for decisions to decide. We only imagine we are resolving a real indeterminacy when we make up our minds; in truth the resolution is eternal. But if eternal, it has no genuine becoming. We say that we "make" a decision; but religious philosophies of being tell us that God makes everything by a single eternal act. So then I make my decision now and God eternally makes it, but if God makes it, how is it my decision rather than God's? Socinus in effect, perhaps without being fully explicit about it, was pointing to the paradox of the double determining of events to which Greek thought in its theological form had led. This brave and honest man had the courage to affirm that we really do make our decisions, and that in so far as we do, God does not make them. We have here the idea of self-creation, which later in Lequier, the French philosopher of a century ago, and still later in William James, Dewey, Whitehead, Sartre, and others has been so often stressed. Note that in Sarte, it was a theological idea before it was an atheistic idea, but if we, and not God, make our decisions, in what fashion can God know these decisions? God cannot decree them in eternity and, by knowing this decree, know what they are, but must perceive them as they occur, and then preserve them in memory. Events—at least those events which are free acts—come into being, are created, at a given time; to know them beforehand—even more, to know them eternally—is a logical absurdity, for it is not beforehand, much less eternally, that they exist to be known. Only as and after they occur are there any such entities to be known. Hence, that God "fails" to know them eternally or is not properly a failure, for success here is mere nonsense, and where

114

success is nonsense, "failure" is inapplicable. Hence, it is quibbling to call God "ignorant" because of things which are not there to be known. This argument was hinted at much earlier (in Cicero, if not before), but the Socinians were the first to make serious theological use of it. They courageously admitted real change in the divine knowledge, the becoming of new knowledge in God to harmonize with the becoming or creation of new things to be known. There is no total creation for God to know in one finally complete act of knowing. Rather, the totality of the real is enriched each moment by as many acts of freedom as occur in the world. With the growth of reality must come a growth of divine knowledge of reality. All this is somewhat further clarified by Lequier three centuries later, followed by Whitehead, who apparently knew little of his predecessors in this way of thinking.

It is notable that the earliest theist of all, Ikhnaton of Egypt, spoke of God's fashioning himself. Thus, self-creation is an old religious idea. One can find it also in ancient India. Medieval antiprocess theology may eventually be seen as but an interlude, a detour from which religious thought has happily returned to the main highway, and clearly, if Socinus allows us to determine part of the content of the divine knowledge by our self-creation, he can hardly wish to deny self-creation to deity. If God is to change, it surely should be in part voluntarily and not solely as result of our initiative. Besides, our self-creativity, like all of our traits, can only be an imperfect image of what in God must be perfect. So there must be an "Eminent" or divine self-creation, of which ours is but a remote and inferior analogue. If, in making our decisions, we make something of ourselves, then analogously God in making supreme decisions, must in some supreme sense be self-created. Even Lequier seems not to see this implication of the process doctrine. Whitehead is our first great systematic philosopher to see it with any great clarity, but the German psychologist and religious thinker, Fechner, had said something like it in his *Zend-Avesta*.

One can, to be sure, read a sort of process philosophy into Hegel and Schelling, but in these writers there are so many concessions to, or echoes of, Greek thought that dispute concerning their classification is to my mind rather unrewarding. They are process philosophers perhaps—if they are anything clear and unambiguous. But what a big "if" this is! They doubtless helped to do away with the classical metaphysics of being; but that they constructed a viable alternative is much less clear.

Socinus and Lequier attacked the theological center of the philosophy of being and absoluteness and proposed a definite alternative, but they failed to generalize this alternative. Only human freedom (and God's knowledge of us) was clearly taken out of the old context; the rest of nature could still be looked upon as unfree, and as subject to immutable divine knowledge. This is where Bergson and Whitehead, preceded at least vaguely by Fechner, come in. Bergson treats all life as to some extent free or creative, and definitely hints, in his later works, that all nature is to some extent free. In Whitehead this implication is made sharply explicit. Not only is each human being a "self-created creature" but every individual is, in some slight degree at least, self-creative, a maker of its own decisions, and so of itself. Divinity is the eminent or supreme form of self-creation, anything else is an inferior form. Whitehead combines this with the Socinian insight that a self-creative creature must also create something in God, for we who make something in ourselves make something in the knowledge of all those who know us, and so make them to a certain extent. We make our friends and enemies just in so far as we are free and they know us. It could not be otherwise, given the essential meanings of "free" and "know." Since God knows all creatures, and a creature is merely an inferior case of what in God is supreme self-creativity, all creatures whatsoever are in part creators of something in God. Whitehead refers to God as Creature, or to the divine Consequent Nature—God as consequent upon or partly created by the world. This is how deity must be conceived in a consistent metaphysics of process.

Whitehead is not indulging in eccentricity at this point, he is merely following out the logic of the decision to make creative becoming the universal category. So when he tells us that creativity is the "category of the ultimate," the "universal of universals," he is summing up and crowning a long development. Freedom is the essence of reality, not a mere special case. To be is to create oneself and thereby to influence the self-creation of those by whom one is known, including God.

Process philosophy, fully thought out, is creationism. Multitudes have talked about God's "creating" of the world, but they usually had no philosophical category adequate to express this idea. All they could do was to say that God was "cause" and the world the effect. They were unable to show in our ordinary experiences of causation any unambiguously creative aspect. The potter shapes the clay, they said, but the supreme Potter, they also said, had shaped the lesser potter completely, and the only genuine decision was the supreme Potter's. Thus, free creation as genuine decision is banished from the world. But how, from such a world, could we possibly form the conception of divine creation? I believe that three thousand years of speculation have led to this result, foreshadowed by Ikhnaton at the outset: creativity, if real at all, must be universal, not limited to God alone, and it must be self-creativity as well as creative influencing of others. In the hymns of Ikhnaton there is nothing about mere causality, nothing about inexorable causal relationships, nothing—unless a vague hint or two—about God's determining the details of the creature's actions. The suggestion almost throughout is of free creatures responding to divine freedom, influencing God to delight in the spectacle they afford for Deity, while they delight in the divine beneficent influence upon them. It took three millennia to change this purely poetic and intuitive vision into a sharply defined philosophical doctrine. Many formidable obstacles had first to be overcome.

Let us look at some of these obstacles. There is the commonsense view, enshrined in European language that the most concrete realities to which abstractions are to be applied, the real "subjects" which have "predicates" are things, individuals which change from one actual state to another—a person, a tree, a mountain, a star—not happenings. There is something more concrete than an individual, and that is the actual history of the individual, the succession of "states," for instance, experiences, which constitute the reality of the individual through time. Is it not clear that the entire actuality of the individual is in one's states, bodily and mental? True, one's possibilities are not exhaustively realized by these states; we could have had other experiences; but we are not now asking what we potentially are, only what we actually have been up to now. The sole way to distinguish the individual from the happenings making up her or his history is in terms of possibility versus actuality, with the states constituting the entire actuality. Are not the actual and the concrete the same? Only in abstract terms can one speak of possible happenings; concrete happenings, knowable as such, and actual happenings are one and the same. Hence, those who take individuals to be wholly concrete will, if they are clear-headed, be forced, with Leibniz, to identify the individual with the total succession of her or his states, but then we do not know who a person is until he or she is dead; we cannot speak of capability of having done (or experienced) something else; for, as Leibniz said, it would not have been that individual but another who would have done it. The commonsense meaning of individual is destroyed if we simply identify an individual with an actual event-sequence. To save this meaning, and we need it for many purposes, we must admit, with the Buddhists and Whitehead, that individuality is somewhat abstract, compared to an actual event-sequence. It is the person now, the present actual state, that "has" the person as the same individual from birth to death, not the same individual that "has" the present actual state. We speak of someone's being "in a state," not of the state as being in the individual. Whitehead can take this literally; substance philosophers cannot. The point is not that individual identity is an illusion, but that it is abstract. Concretely there is a new person each moment, "born anew" in religious language. Of course, in many important personality traits it may be the same person all the time. Each new state fits onto the one series which started with a certain embryo state in a certain mother. It is always, while the person lives, the same series, but the identity of such a series is somewhat abstract. To see the person as always the very same entity, we must abstract from what is new in the individual at each moment. Personal identity through experiences is a property of the experiences, not properties of the identity, or of the ego. If they were, to know an individual would mean knowing all her or his future. We should not really know which individual was John or Joan until John or Joan was dead. This is not how we use the idea of self-identity. It took European philosophy over two thousand years to think through this issue, an issue which Buddhism thought through long ago. Contemporary physics, with its view of reality as consisting in events related in the four dimensions of space-time, helped Whitehead to see the point, but the Buddhists got there without this help.

The argument against the process view has been, "If there is change, something, X, must have changed from state A to state B." Very well, suppose the weather changes from wet to dry, does this mean there is an entity, the weather, as concrete as the wet and dry states? Are these "in" the weather? Surely the weather is in them. Suppose "public opinion" changes, or "the situation" changes—is it not obvious that the "subjects of change" here are relatively abstract entities? Process philosophy generalizes this insight, treating change as the successive becoming of events related to one another, but also differing from one another in some more or less abstract respects which interest us. Change is the becoming of novelty, and process philosophy is all for that.

Another argument states that memory shows us that we, the very same persons, were there in the past having certain experiences. But again, no one denies personal self-identity, provided its abstractness or partial nature is recognized. In the past that I recall, "I" was there, just in so far as what is important about "my" personal sequence of experiences was already in the earlier experiences, but why is it that we cannot remember our identical selves as small infants? Surely because in those early states what is now most important about us was not yet actual. To abstract from all that we have become since early infancy is more than we can do and still leave anything worth distinctly recalling as ourselves. Even in fairly early childhood important personality traits were already beginning to emerge, and so we can recall childhood experiences as making us already the "same" person we are now. Still, we certainly cannot ever remember that in the past we were concretely and precisely what we are now, for that we were not. The "self-same ego" is an abstraction from concrete realities, not itself a fully concrete reality. To see this is the beginning of wisdom in the theory of selfhood. The Buddhists saw it. Did the Hindus? I am not convinced they did.

One of the many signs of confusion in substance philosophy is the failure to deal with the obvious logical truth that identity is a symmetrical relation: if X is Y, then Y is X. Very well, if identity explains memory of the past, by the same token it does not explain the failure to "remember" the future. If memory is an entity being, or intuiting, that very same entity, then it ought to work equally in both directions. In spite of claims of some students of psychical research, the lack of real symmetry in this respect is too glaring to be ignored. We anticipate trends, extrapolate them into the future, but we remember not trends but particular incidents. Identity is not the logical structure to express this and that substance philosophers rarely even mention this point is proof enough of how far they are from clarity as to the real problems. As Whitehead says, identity is "exactly the wrong answer" if the question is, "how do we explain the creativity of process, its production of novelty?" That it is the same entity does not imply that there are new states of the entity, still less that it is the previous states which are experienced, not the subsequent ones. In general, all attempts to explain becoming as a special case of being, novelty as a special case of permanence, have failed. Becoming is said to be a mixture of being and not-being; this is so incomplete a statement as to be less than a half-truth. Becoming is not simply a mixture of being and not-being, it is a mixture of which a new substance is created every moment, but in this moment by moment creation of new cases of being-not-being is the whole mystery of becoming. A fixed mixture of what is and what is not would still not be becoming but at most only a deficient form of being. The becoming of new, allegedly deficient forms of being is simply becoming, and no light is thrown on the transition to novelty by the talk about being and its negation. We shall see that, by contrast, being can very well be explicated as an aspect of becoming, permanence as an aspect of novelty. The converse procedure has always failed, though people have often refused to take note of the failure. When they noted it, they excused themselves by declaring becoming "unreal." Its refusal to subordinate itself to being condemned it. This is sheer question-begging. The necessity of the subordination having been assumed, of course it could also be deduced, but the validity of the assumption is not thereby confirmed; rather the resistance of becoming to the attempted subordination disconfirms the theory.

An important obstacle to the process view is the apparent continuity of becoming—for instance, of experiencing. It seems that experiencing is not a succession of distinct acts or happenings but just one perpetually changing act or happening, at least between waking and sleeping. Here some process philosophers have stopped short and never reached full clarity. This applies to Bergson and Dewey, for instance. Here again Whitehead, preceded by the Buddhists, and to his great credit by William James, carried the analysis through. Continuity is an abstract mathematical concept, not a given actuality. Half a continuum is itself a smaller continuum but half a person is not a smaller person, nor is half a molecule just a smaller molecule. If happenings are actualities, and even more concrete than individuals, they must be like molecules or people, not like mathematical schema. If experiencing were continuous, then half of a half of a half . . . of an experience would also be an experience. However, though in a tenth of a second we can have an experience, in half of a half of a half of a tenth, it seems we cannot. Were we experiencing a continuum, indeed, we should have an infinite number of experiences between waking and having breakfast. This seems quite absurd, but the alternative is that we have a finite number of experiences, and no finite number can make a continuum. James said that each "specious present" was a new unit happening which comes into actuality as a whole, not bit by bit. Whitehead accepts this, and generalizes it for other types of experiencing than the human, and ultimately for all happenings whatever. Reality consists of the becoming of unit events, which he calls "actual entities," "actual occasions," "drops of experience." It is only with this doctrine that process philosophy can effectively compete with substance philosophies, for these had the advantage that individuals, at least individual animals, are units such that half a unit is not a unit in the same sense at all. In a room, the number of persons can be definite and finite; but in process philosophies which admit continuity, the number of happenings, even of a given kind, must be infinite in a single second, but then all definiteness is lost, and there are no objective units of reality. Giving up continuity—and here, too, Whitehead was helped by physics, with its quanta, while the Buddhists got there unaided—the difficulty is overcome. True, we cannot perhaps know what corresponds, in other animals and other types of process than human experiencing, to the human specious present of about .1 second. However, in some cases, e.g., birds, we can rather safely posit a greater number of experiences than ten while a clock ticks off one second. In any case this is a question of detail only.

Another difficulty which a process philosopher must deal with is the requirement that his or her view must not mean that literally "everything changes," or as the Buddhists put it, "everything is impermanent," passes away, from which they deduced the unimportance of ordinary human concerns. In meditation, in mysterious Nirvana, the Buddhists felt that they somehow transcended even impermanence, but only in nonrational fashion. It is necessary for a philosopher to have also a more theoretical escape. Buddha hinted once that there was something which does not pass away, but this was about as far as he would go. Here Bergson, along with Peirce, and then most explicitly and clearly Whitehead, has a great addition to make to the tradition of process philosophy. How do we even know that things have passed away, if not by preserving in memory at least something of what they have been? In memory, past happenings are still somehow with us. Moreover, in perception also, past happenings in a fashion linger on in present experience. We now hear the explosion which in fact took place some seconds ago; we see a stellar explosion which took place years in the past. Memory and perception both somehow embrace the past and preserve something at least of its character. In human memory and perception this "immortality of the past" is faint and fragmentary; but then all human capacities are imperfect, limited. If we are to raise the question of deity at all, why not consider a perfect or divine memory and a perfect or divine perception of happenings, once they have occurred? In such a perfect memory or perception the past might be literally immortal, adequately preserved in all its quality, all its beauty, forever.

Is this merely introducing God as a trick device to rid us of our difficulties? What can any theory do but explain what otherwise remains inexplicable? It is no simple emotional need that events should be preserved, that our lives should forever have some place or function in reality after they are over, or after, perhaps, all human life is ended. It is also a logical demand that after events have happened, it should always be true that they have. If the Buddhists are right, what can make it true that things have happened just as they have? Truth must be true of reality. If the reality keeps fading out, so must truth, but what then would make it true that it had faded? Thus, the literal immortality of the past, in principle accounted for by memory and perception but adequately only in an adequate memory or perception, is required to explain what "truth" means.

One can justify introducing the idea of God into process philosophy in still other ways. I shall deal only with the following. If self-creativity is the universal principle, if all actualities are partly self-determined or free, what prevents indefinitely great confusion and conflict? Confusion and conflict are indeed real, but they are limited. The cosmos does go on in a reasonably foreseeable way, countless sorts of processes fit together into a varied and beautiful whole and nobody thinks the universe is likely to blow up in universal conflict. The cosmic order can be viewed in one of two ways: first, the many self-created creatures harmonize together sufficiently to constitute a cosmos, not thanks to any controlling influence or guidance, but purely spontaneously. Either by sheer luck or their own unimaginable wisdom and goodness, they cooperate to constitute and maintain a viable cosmos. Secondly, the many self-created creatures harmonize together to constitute a viable cosmos thanks to some controlling influence or guidance. This influence or guidance can, in a process philosophy, consist only in a supreme form of self-creative power, a supreme form of process which, because of its superiority, exerts an attraction upon all the others or, as Whitehead likes to put it, "persuades" or "lures" them to follow its directive. I believe a strong case indeed can be made for the latter, against the former. This is the "argument from design" or from order, as process philosophy conceives it.

You can read the great critics of the theistic proofs—Hume and Kant—but you will not find that they have any clear conception of the argument in this form. For example, they object that the order of the world, as we know it at least, is far from perfect, but process philosophy does not presume that there is an absolute order but only that, whatever disorder there may be in the cosmos, it is a thinkable cosmos, rather than an unthinkable chaos or confusion, and of course the order is not absolute if all creatures are partly self-determined. They respond to the universal lure or directive, but it is they who respond, and just how they respond is in some measure their own decision. Though they can cause one another suffering by unfortunate responses, they cannot really disrupt the universe. Were there no universal directive, there seems no way to understand such an invulnerable integrity of the universe. If it be said that we do not know this integrity to obtain, the reply is, it does not matter whether we know it or merely have faith in it, for to such faith there is no feasible alternative. Life itself is a venture of faith in the orderliness of reality. Only verbally can we renounce this faith, but some of us value, as a precious luxury if nothing more, the possibly of a rational theory of that orderliness. Theism alone can furnish such a theory. The rest is simply a mystery.

I wish to deal now with a central doctrine of Whitehead, that in the creative act which is reality itself "the many become one and are increased by one." To see what this means one may take one's own momentary experience as illustration. An experience is a unit happening, and we have new ones about ten times a second, but they fit together so smoothly that we do not distinctly notice the transitions. In such a unit experience there are memories of preceding experiences, especially those in the previous second or less, and there are various perceptions. Whatever is remembered and whatever is perceived also consists, from the most concrete point of view, in unit happenings, analogous to single human experiences. The perceived or remembered happenings are the "many" referred to in the above quotation. That they "become one" is slightly elliptical, for "they are embraced together in a new unit reality," the experience in question but the multiplicity of events has thereby been "increased by one," as is obvious. In the next moment this event, too, will be remembered or perceived, and so "become one" with various other events. Thus, the process of experiencing is a perpetual unification of a pluralistic reality which, as fast as it gets unified, becomes pluralistic again, and so can never be finally unified. Process is creative synthesis, the many into a new one producing a new many—and so on forever. The synthesis is creative, for how could a plurality dictate its own increase? Determinism, if carried to the limit, is magic, not rationality. The causal conditions for each free act are previous acts of freedom; creativity feeds upon its own products and upon nothing else. Whitehead's "eternal objects" may seem to contradict this; if they do, then I should reject them. Because the previous products are retained in the new syntheses, there is, in spite of Buddhism, any amount of permanence in this philosophy. The products of creation are never destroyed by new creation, but always utilized and preserved forever, at least on the divine level.

What Whitehead calls the "principle of relativity" is the principle of creativity looked at in reverse, as it were. Whatever in any sense is, he says, furnishes a "potential" for all subsequent acts of synthesis. "Being" is defined here through becoming. That may be said to be which is available for memory or perception, for integration into ever new acts of synthesis, and in this sense is a potential for all future becoming. To be is to be available for all future actualities. This availability is the very meaning of present "reality." There are profound ethical and religious implications of this view which Buddhism (though without giving a clear rationale for them) appreciated, and Whitehead also emphasizes. I call the doctrine "contributionism." Individual existence is nothing more nor less than a contribution to the future world society, the entire life and value of which is destined to be appreciated and enjoyed forever by the Eminent or Divine creativity, this immortality in God being the creatures' only value in the long run. Egocentric motivations essentially consist in metaphysical confusion. This is why a Buddhist termed the egocentric view "writhing in delusion," for it involves one in an utterly vain and painful attempt to make reality ultimately a contribution to oneself; whereas the final destiny and value of all nondivine life lies beyond the particular self.

The foregoing doctrine literally defines "being," or permanent reality, in terms of becoming. Thus, it is a misconception to suppose that process philosophy, siding with becoming, rejects being. Rather, it is a doctrine of being in becoming, permanence in the novel; by contrast, philosophies of being are doctrines of becoming in being, novelty in the permanent. The trouble is that to insinuate anything new into the permanent is to make it a new thing. The old with the least new factor is, as a whole, new. This is inherent in the meaning of "whole," that its parts contribute to it; and with new parts making new contributions there must to that extent be a new whole. Only abstractly, by disregarding the new, can we say that it is the very same whole, but then it becomes a relative and partly subjective matter how far the new is worthy of being disregarded in this fashion. What is not relative or subjective is the logical necessity that in its concrete entirety the whole reality is always new, however unimportant the novel additions. The only clear alternative to this is Leibniz's denial that in reality anything new is ever added, since the individual contained all his adventures the moment he was born or created. It is a fine example of how little people want to speak precisely that nearly everyone in philosophy has thought he could reject Leibniz's proposal without going on to a philosophy of events and without giving up the meaning of individual needed in ordinary speech (that of an entity identifiable in abstraction from many particular facts about it) and do all this without confusion or inconsistency. Leibniz saw with deadly accuracy the real issue—

what does the concretely definite include in this definiteness? If the concretely definite is the individual as identical throughout his career, then at all times the individual's adventures, past and future, are parts of the individual. If the concretely definite is not the individual but the momentary states, then there can be a real distinction between present, past, and future, otherwise not. Leibniz never thought of taking this process view, but he did see once for all the impossibility of having it both ways, that is, taking the enduring individual as the definite or concrete entity and also supposing that the given individual might, as that same individual, take this course or that, make this decision or that, enjoy this experience or that. The common sense meaning of individual as facing real alternatives is incompatible with the metaphysics which takes the most concrete units of reality to be enduring individuals; it is only consistent with a metaphysics which takes momentary states to be the concrete realities. That this is not a commonplace in philosophy is an illustration of cultural lag. Leibniz gave us our chance to be clear about the point; it is time we took advantage of his contribution.

So far from its being true that Whitehead, for instance, is denying our right to talk of persons as self-identical through change, he is rather protecting this right against the threat of a metaphysics which fails to harmonize with it except thanks to vagueness or ambiguity. There is a somewhat abstract identity of persons and enduring objects. This is just the point, that identity through change is abstractly real. Also, persons and things are almost concrete, they are concrete in comparison with obviously abstract entities such as "being human" or "triangle." Aristotelian substantialism was vaguely and roughly correct; Leibniz was precisely and with the clarity of genius wrong; Whitehead is as clear as Leibniz, but faithful to the indispensable elements of the notion of enduring individuality.

The reader may have been worried about the way in which I have taken human experience as the model of reality. Is this not suspiciously anthropomorphic? The answer is, I have taken human experience only as one end of an analogy which may be stretched as wide as one's imagination can stretch it. An amoeba can "learn" and make what look like "choices" or exhibit "strategy" toward a "desired" end. Of course its "experiences" or "feelings" are not much like ours, but to say that they are absolutely different, or (the same) that it has none, is merely to say that we cannot have the faintest idea of what it is like to be an amoeba, or that we can only know about an amoeba what it looks like to a human being observing it. Similarly, we can perhaps only know what a molecule is as a humanly perceived phenomenon, but cannot know what it is to be a molecule. We can know it as an element in an event of human experience but not as an event on its own. Whitehead does not deny that one may play safe in this way, but he thinks it is a sheer illusion to suppose that there is some other way to try to conceive what an amoeba or atom is in itself than to try to imagine how it feels. He finds no other way, and neither do I. A fair number of philosophers and scientists, from Leibniz down to our time, have agreed with us. The greatest process philosophers have been universal psychicalists, seeing in mind or experience "the sole self-intelligible thing" (Peirce); in this, agreeing with the last great philosopher of being (Leibniz). They find no reasonable explanation of "matter," except as a form or manifestation of "mind." Metaphysics has always tended to reach this result. Northern Buddhism illustrates this, but so does Hinduism and it is only a little below the surface in Plato and Aristotle. The opponents of psychicalistic metaphysics are, whether they know it or not, opponents of all metaphysics, for no clear metaphysical alternative has ever been proposed. Dualism is a problem, not a solution. That experiences do occur cannot be denied; hence, the only open question is, does anything else occur? One may safely defy critics to prove the affirmative. Nonhuman experiences occur, no doubt, but that things constituted by no sort of experience, however different from ours, occur—this no science, no philosophy, can possibly establish. An intelligible world—picture results from so modulating the idea of experience as such that it coincides with that of reality. At no lesser price can such a picture be had.

Neoclassical metaphysics is the fusion of the idealism or psychicalism which is implicit or explicit in all metaphysics with the full realization of the primacy of becoming as self-creativity or creative synthesis, feeding only upon its own products forever. This creativity may be conceived to have an eminent or divine form as well as lesser forms, and it perpetually immortalizes its products, literally so by virtue of the eminent creativity. In no other philosophy, I believe, have so many theoretical and spiritual values been united with so much appearance of consistency and clarity. If this is not so, then I am indeed deluded.

CHARLES HARTSHORNE: PRIMARY BIBLIOGRAPHY OF PHILOSOPHICAL WORKS

Compiled by Dorothy C. Hartshorne

Revised and Updated by Donald Wayne Viney and Randy Ramal

Copyrighted by *Process Studies*,
Volume 30.2, Fall-Winter, 2001 (374-409).

Permission to publish in print and on Harvard Square Library
website granted by the editor, Barry L. Whitney

This bibliography is a corrected version of the one that appeared in *Process Studies* 30, 2 (2001): 374-409. Earlier versions appeared in *Process and Divinity*, the Hartshorne Festschrift, eds, William L. Reese and Eugene Freeman (La Salle, Illinois: Open Court, 1964): 579-591; *Process Studies* 6, 1 (1973): 73-93 [Addenda published in issue 11, 2 (1981): 108-13]; and in *The Philosophy of Charles Hartshorne*, the Library of Living Philosophers, volume XX, ed. Lewis Hahn (La Salle, Illinois: Open Court, 1991): 735-66. Randy Ramal, at the Center for Process Studies, added material to these earlier works in his alphabetically ordered bibliographies of Hartshorne's works posted on the CPS web site. Don Viney, working independently, was also adding items to the LLP bibliography. The following combines our separate efforts and is more than what either of us produced individually. We have added missing items, corrected typographical mistakes, and included cross-references for articles that later appeared in Hartshorne's books.

Although we followed Dorothy Hartshorne's practice of listing items in chronological order, we diverged from her lead by (1) listing Hartshorne's abstracts of his books and articles under the same item as the book or article itself; (2) listing reviews and articles, including translations, that appeared in more than one place—but not in one of Hartshorne's books—under a single heading; (3) listing multiple replies in a single volume under a single item (Dorothy did this, but inconsistently). Thus, forty-eight items that she listed separately are consolidated here under other entries.[1]

This bibliography revises and updates Dorothy's original, but it is in one respect less than what she compiled, for no attempt is made to list Hartshorne's ornithological works unless they include philosophical content. Moreover, we make no claim to being exhaustive; for example, a complete bibliography would include Hartshorne's many letters to the editor, but none of those are listed here (nor are they listed in the bibliographies mentioned above). It is worth noting that there are over sixty unpublished articles in the Hartshorne archives, as well as a substantial portion of the last book he planned and an extensive correspondence. Thus, what is offered here, though more extensive than previous bibliographies, is nevertheless a work in progress.[2]

Books

1.   *Collected Papers of Charles Sanders Peirce*. Edited by Charles Hartshorne and Paul Weiss. Cambridge: Harvard UP.

> Vol. 1, *Principles of Philosophy*, 1931.
> Vol. 2, *Elements of Logic*, 1932.
> Vol. 3, *Exact Logic*, 1933.
> Vol. 4, *The Simplest Mathematics*, 1933.
> Vol. 5, *Pragmatism and Pragmaticism*, 1934.
> Vol. 6, *Scientific Metaphysics*, 1935.

2.   *The Philosophy and Psychology of Sensation*. Chicago: U of Chicago P, 1934. Reissued in Port Washington, New York: Kennikat P, 1968.

3.   *Beyond Humanism: Essays in the New Philosophy of Nature*. Chicago: Willet, Clark and Company, 1937. Reprinted as a Bison Book Edition, with new Preface. Lincoln: U of Nebraska P, 1968. Also reprinted in Gloucester, Massachusetts: Peter Smith, 1975.

4.   *Man's Vision of God and the Logic of Theism*. Chicago: Willet, Clark and Company, 1941. After 1948 published by Harper and Brothers, New York. Reprinted by Hamden, Connecticut: Archon Books, 1964.

5.   *The Divine Relativity: A Social Conception of God*. The Terry Lectures, 1947. New Haven: Yale UP, 1948.

6.   *Whitehead and the Modern World: Science, Metaphysics, and Civilization, Three Essays on the Thought of Alfred North Whitehead*. By Victor Lowe, Charles Hartshorne, and A.H. Johnson. Boston: the Beacon P, 1950. "Whitehead's Metaphysics" by Charles Hartshorne, 25-41. Reprinted by Books for Libraries P, 1972. "Whitehead's Metaphysics" reprinted as chapter 2 of *Whitehead's Philosophy*. See abstract in Program of the American Philosophical Association, Western Division (May 6-8, 1948): 13-14.

7.   *Reality as Social Process: Studies in Metaphysics and Religion*. Foreword by William Ernest Hocking. Glencoe: The Free P and Boston: The Beacon P, 1953. Reprinted in New York: Hafner Publishing Co., 1971.

8.   *Philosophers Speak of God* (with William L. Reese). Chicago: U of Chicago P, 1953, reprinted in 1969. Reissued by Chicago: Midway Reprints, 1976. Reprinted by Amherst, New York: Humanity Books, 2000, with an addendum to the Preface by William L. Reese.

9.   *The Logic of Perfection and Other Essays in Neoclassical Metaphysics*. La Salle, Illinois: Open Court, 1962. Author's abstract in *The Monist* 59, 4 (1976): 596.

10.   *Anselm's Discovery: A Re-Examination of the Ontological Proof for God's Existence*. La Salle, Illinois: Open Court, 1965.

11.   The Social Conception of the Universe [Three chapters from Reality as Social Process]. Edited by Keiji Matsunobu. Tokyo: Aoyama, and New York: Macmillan, 1967.

12.   *A Natural Theology for Our Time*. La Salle, Illinois: Open Court, 1967. Author's abstract in *The Monist* 59, 4 (1976): 594.

13.   *Creative Synthesis and Philosophic Method*. London: SCM P Ltd., and La

Salle, Illinois: Open Court, 1970. Reprinted in 1983 by Lanham, Maryland: UP of America. Chinese translation in process (The China Project, Center for Process Studies, Claremont, California). Author's abstract in *The Monist* 56, 4 (1972): 626-27.

14.   *Whitehead's Philosophy: Selected Essays, 1935-1970.* Lincoln: U of Nebraska P, 1972. [Japanese translation by Keiji Matsunobu and Minoru Otsuka, Kyoto: Korosha, 1989.]

15.   *Born to Sing: An Interpretation and World Survey of Bird Song.* Bloomington: Indiana UP, 1973. Author's abstract in *The Monist* 59, 2 (1976): 299.

16.   *Aquinas to Whitehead: Seven Centuries of Metaphysics of Religion. The Aquinas Lecture, 1976.* Milwaukee: Marquette U Publications, 1976.

17.   *Whitehead's View of Reality* (with Creighton Peden). New York: Pilgrim P, 1981. "Whitehead in Historical context" by Charles Hartshorne, 2-24.

18.   *Insights and Oversights of Great Thinkers: An Evaluation of Western Philosophy.* Albany: State U of New York P, 1983.

19.   *Omnipotence and other Theological Mistakes.* Albany: State U of New York P, 1984. [Japanese translation by Minoru Otsuka. Kyoto: Korosha, 1991.] Author's abstract in *The Monist* 69, 4 (1986): 633.

20.   *Creativity in American Philosophy.* Albany: State U of New York P, 1984. [Spanish translation by Mari Luz Caso as *Creatividad en la Filosofia Estadonnidense* (Mexico: Edamex, 1987).]

21.   *Wisdom as Moderation: A Philosophy of the Middle Way.* Albany: State U of New York P, 1987. [Japanese translation by Minoru Otsuka, with a preface by Charles Hartshorne.]

22.   *The Darkness and the Light: A Philosopher Reflects Upon His Fortunate Career and Those Who Made It Possible.* Albany: State U of New York P, 1990.

23.   *The Zero Fallacy and Other Essays in Neoclassical Philosophy.* Edited and Introduced by Mohammad Valady. Peru, Illinois: Open Court, 1997.

24.   *Hartshorne and Brightman on God, Process, and Persons: The Correspondence, 1922-1945.* Edited by Randall E. Auxier and Mark Y. A. Davies. Nashville: Vanderbilt UP, 2001.

25.   *The Unity of Being.* [Original title: *An Outline and Defense of the Argument for the Unity of Being in the Absolute or Divine Good*]. Doctoral Dissertation, Harvard University. (May 1923). Edited by Randall E. Auxier and Hyatt Carter. Forthcoming from Open Court, 2003.

Articles, Reviews, and Discussions

1.   "Memory, Youth, and Age." *The Haverfordian* 37, 8 (1916): 323.

2.   "Barriers to Progress: Or Some Superstitions of Modernism." *The Gad-Fly* [Student Liberal Club of Harvard University] (1923): 1-15.

3.   Review of A.N. Whitehead. *Symbolism, Its Meaning and Effect* (New York: Macmillan, 1927). *Hound and Horn* 1 (1927): 148-52.

4.   Reviews of Martin Heidegger. *Sein und Zeit*; Oskar Becker, *Mathematische Existenz* (from *Jahrbuch für Philosophie und Phanomenologische Forschung*, Herausgegeben von Edmund Husserl) [Achter Band. Halle: Max Niemeyer, 1927, xxi, 809]. *Philosophical Review* 38, 3 (1929): 284-93. Incorporated into chapter 17

of *Beyond Humanism.*

5.   "Continuity, the Form of Forms, in Charles Peirce." *The Monist* 39, 4 (1929): 521-34.

6.   Review of Etienne Souriau. *L'Avenir de l'esthétique* (Paris: Félix Alcan, 1929). *International Journal of Ethics* 40, 1 (1929): 132-33

7.   "Ethics and the Assumption of Purely Private Pleasures." *International Journal of Ethics* 40, 4 (1930): 496-515.

8.   "Sense Quality and Feeling Tone." *Proceedings of the Seventh International Congress of Philosophy,* ed. Gilbert Ryle (London: Oxford UP, 1931): 168-72.

9.   "Contingency and the New Era in Metaphysics, I." *Journal of Philosophy* 29, 16 (1932): 421-31; "Contingency and the New Era in Metaphysics, II." *Journal of Philosophy* 29, 17 (1932): 457-69.

10.   Review of André Lalande. *Les Illusions évolutionnistes* (Paris: Félix Alcan, 1930). *International Journal of Ethics* 43, 1 (1932): 94-97.

11.   "Four Principles of Method—with Applications." *The Monist* 43, 1 (1933): 40-72.

12.   Review of G. Watts Cunningham. *The Idealistic Argument in Recent British and American Philosophy* (New York: Century, 1933). *International Journal of Ethics* 43, 4 (1933): 447-49.

13.   Foreword to *The Categories of Charles Peirce* by Eugene Freeman (Chicago: Open Court, 1934).

14.   Review of R. G. Collingwood. *An Essay on Philosophical Method* (Oxford: Clarendon, 1933). *International Journal of Ethics* 44, 3 (1934): 357-58.

15.   "The Intelligibility of Sensations." *The Monist* 44, 2 (1934): 161-85.

16.   Reviews of Ernest W. Barnes. *Scientific Theory and Religion* (New York: Macmillan, 1933); J. E. Turner. *Essentials in the Development of Religion* (New York: Macmillan, 1934); T. V. Seshagiro Row. *New Light on Fundamental Problems* (Madras: UP, 1932). *International Journal of Ethics* 44, 4 (1934): 465-71.

17.   Reviews of Gerhard Kraenzlin. *Max Schelers' Phaenomenologische Systematik*; Adolph Sternberger, *Der verstandene Tod* (Leipzig: S. Hirzel, 1934). *International Journal of Ethics* 44, 4 (1934): 478-80.

18.   "Redefining God." *New Humanist* 7, 4 (1934): 8-15. Reprinted in *Contemporary American Protestant Thought: 1900-1970,* ed. William R. Miller (Indianapolis, Indiana: Bobbs-Merrill Co., 1973): 315-322. Also reprinted in *American Journal of Theology and Philosophy* 22, 2 (2001): 107-13.

19.   "The New Metaphysics and Current Problems, I." *New Frontier* 1, 1 (1934): 24-31; "The New Metaphysics and Current Problems, II." *New Frontier* 1, 5 (1934): 8-14.

20.   "Ethics and the New Theology." *International Journal of Ethics* 45, 1 (1934): 90-101.

21.   Review of Louis Vialle. *Le Désir du néant* (Paris: Félix Alcan, 1933). *International Journal of Ethics* 45, 1 (1934): 116-117.

22.   Review of William Pepperell Montague. *The Chances of Surviving Death* (Cambridge: Harvard UP, 1934). *International Journal of Ethics* 45, 1 (1934): 120-21

23. Reviews of John Nibb. *Christianity and Internationalism* (London: Elliot Stock, 1934); Georges Lakhovsky. *Le Racisme et l'orchestre universelle* (Paris: Félix Alcan, 1934). *International Journal of Ethics* 45, 1 (1934): 121-22.

24. "The Parallel Development of Method in Physics and Psychology." *Philosophy of Science* 1, 4 (1934): 446-59.

25. "Pattern and Movement in Art and Science." *Comment* (The U of Chicago) 3, 2 (1935): 1-2, 11. Chapter 2 of *Reality as Social Process*.

26. Discussion: "Flexibility of Scientific Truth." *Philosophy of Science* 2 (1935): 255-56.

27. Review of D. Draghicesco. *Vérité et Revelation*, Vol. 1. (Paris: Félix Alcan, 1934). *International Journal of Ethics* 45, 2 (1935): 248-249. [cf. item 36] Incorporated into chapter 4 of *Beyond Humanism*.

28. Review of Adolphe Ferrière. *Der Primat des Geistes als Grundlage einer aufbauenden Erziehung*, Translated by Emmi Hirschberg (Berlin: Julius Beltz, n.d.). *International Journal of Ethics* 45, 2 (1935): 250.

29. Review of Henry C. Simons. *A Positive Program for Lassaiz Faire* (Chicago: U of Chicago P, 1935). *Christian Century* 52, 23 (1935): 761-62.

30. "Metaphysics for Positivists." *Philosophy of Science* 2, 3 (1935): 287-303.

31. "On Some Criticisms of Whitehead's Philosophy." *Philosophical Review* 44, 4 (1935): 323-44. [cf. item 50]. Chapter 3 of *Whitehead's Philosophy*.

32. Reviews of John Wisdom. *Problems of Mind and Matter* (Cambridge: Cambridge UP, 1934); Thomas Whittaker. *Reason* (Cambridge: Cambridge UP, 1934); Julius W. Friend and James Feibleman. *Science and the Spirit of Man* (London: Allen and Unwin, 1933). *International Journal of Ethics* 45, 4 (1935): 461-65.

33. Review of Gajanan Wasudeo Kaveeshwar. *The Metaphysics of Berkeley Critically Examined in the Light of Modern Philosophy* (Mandleshwar, India: A. Kaveeshwar, 1933). *International Journal of Ethics* 45, 4 (1935): 494.

34. "The Compound Individual." *Philosophical Essays for Alfred North Whitehead*, ed. Otis H. Lee (New York: Longmans Green, 1936): 193-220. Chapter 4 of *Whitehead's Philosophy*.

35. "The New Pantheism, I." *Christian Register* 115, 8 (1936): 119-20; "The New Pantheism, II." *Christian Register* 115, 9 (1936): 141-43.

36. Review of D. Draghicesco. *Vérité et Revelation*, Vol. 2, (Paris: Félix Alcan, 1934). *International Journal of Ethics* 47, 1 (1936): 133-35. [cf. item 27].

37. "The Philosophical Limitations of Humanism." *University Review* 3, 4 (1937): 240-42. Chapter 11 of *Reality as Social Process*.

38. Abstract: "Positivism as Anthropomorphism." *The Journal of Philosophy* 34, 25 (1937): 685.

39. Review of André Cresson. *La Representation*. (Paris: Boivin, 1936). *Philosophical Review* 47, 1 (1938): 90-91.

40. Review of G. P. Adams, W. R. Dennes, J. Loewenberg, D. S. Mackay, P. Marhenke, S. C. Pepper, and E. W. Strong. *Knowledge and Society* (New York: Appleton-Century, 1938). *Christian Century* 55, 30 (1938): 917.

41. Reply to [R. H., Jr.] Randall's review of *Beyond Humanism*, in *Journal of Philosophy* 35, 5 (1938): 131-33.

42. Review of Jacques Maritain. *The Degrees of Knowledge* (New York: Scribner's, 1938). *Christian Century* 55 (1938): 1195. Also in *Journal of Religion* 19, 3 (1939): 267-69.

43. "The Reality of the Past, the Unreality of the Future." *Hibbert Journal* 37, 2 (1939): 246-57.

44. Review of Wilhelm Keller. *Der Sinnbegriff als Kategorie der Geisteswissenschaften* (Munich: Ernst Reinhardt, 1937). *Philosophical Review* 48, 1 (1939): 95.

45. Review of Rasvihari Das. *The Philosophy of Whitehead* (London: James Clarke and Co., 1964). *Philosophical Review* 48, 2 (1939): 230-31.

46. Notes: Letter (Reply to Roger Holmes). *Philosophical Review* 68, 2 (1939): 243.

47. "The Method of Imaginative Variations," in "Notes Concerning Husserl." *Journal of Philosophy* 36, 9 (1939): 233-34.

48. "Are All Propositions about the Future either True or False?" *Program of the American Philosophical Association* (April 20-22, 1939): 26-32.

49. Review of A.N. Whitehead. *Modes of Thought* (New York: Macmillan, 1938). *Review of Religion* 3, 4 (1939): 494-496.

50. Discussion: "The Interpretation of Whitehead (Reply to John W. Blyth)." *Philosophical Review* 48, 4 (1939): 415-23. [cf. item 31].

51. Review of James Bissett Pratt. *Naturalism* (New Haven: Yale UP, 1939). *Journal of Religion* 19, 3 (1939): 234-35.

52. Review of Ralph Barton Perry. *In the Spirit of William James* (New Haven: Yale UP, 1938). *Journal of Religion* 19, 3 (1939): 247-48.

53. Review of A. Campbell Garnett. *Reality and Value* (New Haven: Yale UP, 1937). *The Scroll* 37, 3 (1939): 93-95.

54. "Husserl and the Social Structure of Immediacy." *Philosophical Essays in Memory of Edmund Husserl.* Marvin Farber, ed. (Cambridge: Harvard UP, 1940): 219-30.

55. "Santayana's Doctrine of Essence." *The Philosophy of George Santayana,* ed. Paul Arthur Schilpp. The Library of Living Philosophers, Vol. 2 (Evanston and Chicago: Northwestern UP, 1940): 135-82.

56. "The Three Ideas of God." *Journal of Liberal Religion* 1, 3 (1940): 9-16. Chapter 9 of *Reality as Social Process.*

57. Review of Justus Buchler. *Charles Peirce's Empiricism* (New York: Harcourt, Brace, 1939). *Ethics* 50, 2 (1940): 248.

58. Review of Josef Maier. *On Hegel's Critique of Kant* (New York: Columbia UP, 1939). *Journal of Religion* 20, 1 (1940): 106.

59. Review of Paul Arthur Schilpp, ed. *The Philosophy of John Dewey.* Library of Living Philosophers (Evanston: Northwestern UP, 1939). *Christian Century* 42, 10 (1940): 313-15. Chapter 12 of *Reality as Social Process.*

60. Review of Irwin Edman. *Arts and the Man* (New York: Norton, 1939). *Ethics* 50, 3 (1940): 369-70.

61. Reviews of Arthur Hazard Dakin. *Man the Measure* (Princeton, N. J.: Princeton UP, 1939); Archibald Allan Bowman, *A Sacramental Universe.* (Princeton,

N. J.: Princeton UP, 1939). *Ethics* 50, 3 (1940): 363-66.

62. Review of Milton Karl Munitz. *The Moral Philosophy of Santayana* (New York: Columbia UP, 1939). *Journal of Religion* 20, 2 (1940): 196-98.

63. Review of Charles M. Perry. *Toward a Dimensional Realism* (Norman: U of Oklahoma P, 1939). *Journal of Religion* 20, 2 (1940): 214.

64. Review of Theodore Meyer Greene. *The Arts and the Art of Criticism* (Princeton, N. J.: Princeton UP, 1940). *Ethics* 51, 1 (1940): 116-17.

65. "Whitehead's Idea of God." *The Philosophy of Alfred North Whitehead*, ed. Paul Arthur Schilpp. The Library of Living Philosophers, Vol. 3 (Evanston and Chicago: Northwestern UP, 1941): 513-59. Chapter 5 of *Whitehead's Philosophy*.

66. "Charles Sanders Peirce's Metaphysics of Evolution." *New England Quarterly* 14, 1 (1941): 49-63.

67. "Anthropomorphic Tendencies in Positivism." *Philosophy of Science* 8, 2 (1941): 184-203.

68. Review of Frederick J. E. Woodbridge. *An Essay on Nature* (New York: Columbia UP, 1940). *Ethics* 51, 4 (1941): 488-90.

69. Review of DeWitt H. Parker. *Experience and Substance* (Ann Arbor: U of Michigan P, 1940). *Christian Century* 48, 27 (1941): 864. Also published in *Philosophical Review* 51, 5 (1942): 523-26.

70. "A Critique of Peirce's Idea of God." *Philosophical Review* 50, 5 (1941): 516-23. See also, "Abstracts of Papers to be Read at the Joint Meeting of the Eastern and Western Divisions of the American Philosophical Association, Columbia U, December, 1939." *Journal of Philosophy* 36, 25 (1939): 683-84.

71. Review of Ledger Wood. *The Analysis of Knowledge* (Princeton, N. J.: Princeton UP, 1941). *Philosophy and Phenomenological Research* 2, 1 (1941): 104-08.

72. Review of Gustaf Stromberg. *The Soul of the Universe* (Philadelphia: David McKay P, 1940). *Review of Religion* 5, 3 (1941): 357-60.

73. "A Philosophy of Democratic Defense." *Science, Philosophy, and Religion: Second Symposium* (New York: Conference on Science, Philosophy, and Religion in their Relation to the Democratic Way of Life, Inc. 1942): 130-72.

74. Review of Justus Buchler, ed. *The Philosophy of Peirce: Selected Writings* (New York: Harcourt Brace, 1940). *Philosophical Review* 51, 1 (1942): 92.

75. Review of Etienne Gilson. *God and Philosophy* (New Haven: Yale UP, 1941). *Journal of Religion* 22, 2 (1942): 221-24.

76. "Elements of Truth in the Group-Mind Concept." *Social Research* 9, 2 (1942): 248-65. Chapter 3 of *Reality as Social Process*.

77. Review of Paul Arthur Schilpp, ed. *The Philosophy of Alfred North Whitehead* (Evanston: Northwestern UP, 1941). *Religion in Life* 11, 3 (1942): 469-70. Also published in *Thought* 17, 66 (1942): 545-47.

78. Review of Stephen C. Pepper. *World Hypotheses* (Berkeley: U of California P, 1942). *Ethics* 53, 1 (1942): 73-75.

79. "Organic and Inorganic Wholes." *Philosophy and Phenomenological Research* 3, 2 (1942): 127-136. Notice in *Program of the Fiftieth Anniversary Symposia* (Chicago: U of Chicago P, 1941): 12. Published as "A World of Organisms," chapter 7 of *Logic*

of Perfection. Republished in *Process Philosophy: Basic Writings,* eds. Jack R. Sibley and Pete A.Y. Gunter (Washington D.C.: UP of America, 1978): 275-96.

80.　Comment on "Democracy and the Rights of Man." *Science, Philosophy, and Religion: Second Symposium* (New York: Conference on Science, Philosophy, and Religion, Inc. 1942): 292.

81.　Review of John Blyth. *Whitehead's Theory of Knowledge* (Providence: Brown UP, 1941). *Philosophy and Phenomenological Research* 3, 3 (1943): 372-75.

82.　"Is Whitehead's God the God of Religion?" [Suggested by Ely's book, cf. item 85]. *Ethics* 53, 3 (1943): 219-27. Chapter 6 of *Whitehead's Philosophy.*

83.　Review of Lewis Edwin Hahn. *A Contextualistic Theory of Perception* (Berkeley: U of California P, 1942). *Ethics* 53, 3 (1943): 233.

84.　Review of Campbell Garnett. *A Realistic Philosophy of Religion* (Chicago: Willett Clark, 1942). *Journal of Religion* 23, 3 (1943): 70-71. Also published in *Ethics* 54, 1 (1943): 62-63.

85.　Review of Stephen Lee Ely. *The Religious Availability of Whitehead's God* (Madison: U of Wisconsin P, 1942). *Journal of Liberal Religion* 5, 1 (1943): 55.

86.　Communication, Rejoinder: "Ely on Whitehead." *Journal of Liberal Religion* 5, 2 (1943): 97-100.

87.　Discussion: "Reflections on the Strength and Weakness of Thomism." *Ethics* 54, 1 (1943): 53-57.

88.　Reviews of Jacques Maritain. *Saint Thomas and the Problem of Evil* (Milwaukee: Marquette UP, 1942) and *The Maritain Volume of 'The Thomist'* (New York: Sheed and Ward, 1943). *Ethics* 54, 1 (1943): 53-57.

89.　"A Mathematical Analysis of Theism." *Review of Religion* 8, 1 (1943): 20-38. Revised as epilogue of *Philosophers Speak of God,* 499-514.

90.　Radio Discussion: "How Christians Should Think About Peace." By Edwin Aubrey, Charles Hartshorne, and Bernard Loomer. Pamphlet. Chicago: U of Chicago Round Table (April 9, 1944): 20 pages.

91.　Review of K. R. Sreenivasa Iyengar. *The Metaphysics of Value,* Vol. 1. (Mysore: U of Mysore, 1942). *Ethics* 54, 3 (1944): 230-31.

92.　Review of John Elof Boodin. *Religion of Tomorrow* (New York: Philosophical Library, 1943). *Ethics* 54, 3 (1944): 233-34.

93.　"The Formal Validity and Real significance of the Ontological Argument." *Philosophical Review* 53, 3 (1944): 225-45. [cf. items 101 and 107].

94.　"Philosophy and Orthodoxy." *Ethics* 54, 4 (1944): 295-98.

95.　Review of Werner Jaeger. *Humanism and Theology* (Milwaukee: Marquette UP, 1943). *Journal of Religion* 24, 3 (1944): 230.

96.　"God and Man not Rivals." *Journal of Liberal Religion* 6, 2 (1944): 9-13.

97.　Abstract: "Beauty as Balance of Unity and Variety." In *Proceedings* of The American Society for Aesthetics. First Annual Meeting. Cleveland, Ohio (Sept. 11-13, 1944): 29-30.

98.　Comments on "Philosophical Ideas and Enduring Peace," 557; on "Philosophical Ideas and World Peace," 597; on "In Quest of Worldly Wisdom," 719-721. *Approaches to World Peace, Fourth Symposium,* eds. Lyman Bryson, Louis Finkelstein, and Robert M. MacIver (New York: Conference on Science, Philosophy, and Religion, 1944).

99.   Review of Henry Alonzo Myers. *The Spinoza-Hegel Paradox* (Ithaca: Cornell UP, 1944). *Ethics* 55, 1 (1944): 71-72.

100.   Review of Adhar Chandra Das. *Negative Fact, Negation, and Truth* (Calcutta: Calcutta UP, 1942). *Ethics* 55, 1 (1944): 77.

101.   Discussion: "On Hartshorne's Formulation of the Ontological Argument: A Rejoinder [to Elton]." *Philosophical Review* 54, 1 (1945): 63-65. [cf. items 93 and 107].

102.   Entries in *An Encyclopedia of Religion*, ed. Vergilius Ferm (New York: Philosophical Library, 1945): acosmism; analogy; anthropopathism; Aristotle and Aristotelianism; axiom; Berkeley, George; Carneades; cause; Copernican astronomy; eternal; eternity; ether; etiology, aetiology; foreknowledge, Divine; Gerson, Levi ben; God, as personal; Hume; infinite; Kant, Immanuel; omnipotence; omnipresence; omniscience; panentheism; panlogism; pantheism; Peirce, Charles Sanders; perfect, perfection; Ptolemaic astronomy; Renouvier, Charles; Spencer, Herbert; Spinoza, Benedict; time; transcendence; Whitehead, Alfred North.

103.   Review Article: "Efficient Causality in Aristotle and St. Thomas" by Francis X. Meehan's book of the same title (Washington: Catholic UP, 1940). *Journal of Religion* 25, 1 (1945): 25-32. [cf. item 111].

104.   Review of Rudolf Jordan. *Homo Sapiens Socialis* (South Africa: Central News Agency, 1944). *Ethics* 55, 4 (1945): 312-13.

105.   Review of Jacques Maritain. *The Dream of Descartes* (New York: Philosophical Library, 1944). *Ethics* 55, 4 (1945): 321.

106.   Review of *Vladimir Soloviev's Lectures on Godmanhood* (with Introduction by Peter Zouboff) (New York: International UP, 1944). *Ethics* 55, 4 (1945): 322.

107.   "Professor Hartshorne's Syllogism: Rejoinder [to Elton]." *Philosophical Review* 54, 5 (1945): 506-08. [cf. items 93 and 101].

108.   Review of K. F. Reinhardt. *A Realistic Philosophy* (Milwaukee: Bruce, 1944). *Philosophical Review* 54, 5 (1945): 521-22.

109.   "A New Philosophic Conception of the Universe." *Hibbert Journal* 44, 1 (1945): 14-21. Chapter 1 of *Reality as Social Process*.

110.   Review of Paul Arthur Schilpp, ed. *The Philosophy of Bertrand Russell*. Library of Living Philosophers, Vol. 5. (Evanston: Northwestern UP, 1944). *Journal of Religion* 25, 4 (1945): 280-84. Chapter 13 of *Reality as Social Process*.

111.   Communication: "Reply to Father Meehan." *Journal of Religion* 26, 1 (1946): 54-57. [cf. item 103].

112.   Review of Erich Frank. *Philosophical Understanding and Religious Truth* (London: Oxford UP, 1945). *Review of Religion* 10, 2 (1946): 182-89.

113.   Review of William Ernest Hocking. *Science and the Idea of God* (Chapel Hill: U of North Carolina P, 1944). *Philosophy and Phenomenological Research* 6, 3 (1946): 453-57.

114.   "Relative, Absolute, and Superrelative: A Formal Analysis." *Philosophical Review* 55, 3 (1946): 213-28. Chapter 6 of *Reality as Social Process*.

115.   "The Common Good and the Value Receptacle." *Program of the American Philosophical Association, Western Division* (May 9-11, 1946): 10-11.

116. "Tragic and Sublime Aspects of Christian Love." *Journal of Liberal Religion* 8, 1 (1946): 36-44. Chapter 8 of *Reality as Social Process*.

117. "Theological Values in Current Metaphysics." *Journal of Religion* 26, 3 (1946): 157-67. Chapter 7 of *Reality as Social Process*.

118. "Leibniz's Greatest Discovery." *Journal of the History of Ideas* 7, 4 (1946): 411-21.

119. "Ideal Knowledge Defines Reality: What Was True in Idealism." *Journal of Philosophy* 43, 21 (1946): 573-82. See also: Correction of "Ideal Knowledge Defines Reality." *Journal of Philosophy* 43, 26 (1946): 724.

120. Review of Henri Bergson. *The Creative Mind*. Trans. Mabelle L. Andison (New York: Philosophy Library, 1946). *Journal of Religion* 27, 1 (1947): 64-65.

121. Review of José Ortega y Gasset. *Concord and Liberty* (New York: Norton, 1946). *Christian Century* 64, 7 (1947): 207.

122. Review of Gustav Theodor Fechner. *Religion of a Scientist: Selections from Fechner*, ed. and trans. Walter Lowrie (New York: Pantheon, 1946). *Journal of Religion* 27, 2 (1947): 126-28.

123. Review of Nels F. S. Ferré. *Faith and Reason* (New York: Harper, 1946). *Review of Religion* 11, 4 (1947): 409-13.

124. Review of Martin Foss. *The Idea of Perfection in the Western World* (Princeton, N. J.: Princeton UP, 1946). *Journal of Modern History* 19, 2 (1947): 15.

125. "God as Absolute, Yet Related to All." *Review of Metaphysics* 1, 1 (1947): 24-51.

126. Review of Henry N. Wieman et al. *Religious Liberals Reply* (Boston: Beacon P, 1947). *Christian Register* 126, 9 (1947): 412-13.

127. Review of A. H. Johnson. *The Wit and Wisdom of Whitehead* (Boston: Beacon P, 1947). *Christian Register* 126, 10 (1947): 446.

128. "Two Levels of Faith and Reason." *Journal of Bible and Religion* 16, 1 (1948): 30-38. See also *Program of Week of Work of the National Council on Religion in Higher Education* (1947): 16. Chapter 10 of *Reality as Social Process*.

129. Review of Paul Weiss. *Nature and Man* (New York: Henry Holt, 1947). *Ethics* 58, 2 (1948): 143-44.

130. Review of Campbell Garnett. *God in Us* (Chicago: Willett Clark, 1945). *Ethics* 58, 2 (1948): 151.

131. "The Rationalistic Criterion in Metaphysics." *Philosophy and Phenomenological Research* 8, 3 (1948): 436-47.

132. "Existential Propositions and the Law of Categories." *Fascicule 1, Proceedings of the Tenth International Congress of Philosophy*, eds. E. W. Beth et al. (Amsterdam: North-Holland Publishing Company, 1948): 342-44.

133. "Aesthetics of Color." *Program: Research in Textiles, Clothing, and Related Art* (March 19-20, 1948): 2.

134. Review of Jean Wahl. *The Philosopher's Way* (New York: Oxford UP, 1948). *Philosophical Review* 57, 5 (1948): 509-11.

135. "Ein theologisches Paradoxon. I Die Wissensform des Paradoxons. II Die Willensform des Paradoxons." *Philosophisches Jahrbuch* 59, 2 (1949): 250-51.

136. "Noch einmal die Zuf,lligkeit der Welt und Notwendigkeit Gottes:

Erwiderung an Dr. Ferdinand Bergenthal." *Philosophisches Jahrbuch* 59, 2 (1949): 355-56.

137. "Ob Göttliches Wissen um die weltliche Existenz notwendig sein kann: Eine Erwiderung." *Philosophisches Jahrbuch* 60, 4 (1950): 469-71.

138. "The Synthesis of Idealism and Realism." *Theoria* (Sweden) 15 (1949): 90-107. Chapter 4 of *Reality as Social Process*; chapter 8, section B of *Zero Fallacy*.

139. "Chance, Love, and Incompatibility." Presidential Address, Western Division of the American Philosophical Association meeting at Columbus, Ohio, April 29, 1949. *Philosophical Review* 58, 5 (1949): 429-50. Chapter 5 of *Reality as Social Process*.

140. Review of Otis Lee. *Existence and Inquiry* (Chicago: U of Chicago P, 1949). *Review of Metaphysics* 3, 1 (1949): 107-14.

141. "Panpsychism." *A History of Philosophical Systems*, ed. Vergilius Ferm (New York: Philosophical Library, 1950): 442-53.

142. "Le Principe de relativité philosophique chez Whitehead." *Revue de Métaphysique et de Morale* 55, 1 (1950): 16-29. Lecture originally delivered at the Sorbonne, Feb. 4, 1949, announced in Bulletin. EC 1959.

143. "The Divine Relativity and Absoluteness: A Reply [to John Wild]." *Review of Metaphysics* 4, 1 (1950): 31-60.

144. "God in General Philosophical Thought." *The Encyclopedia Hebraica* 3 (1951) [Jewish Calendar 5711], Jerusalem: Encyclopedia Publishing Company, 1951: 467-78.

145. "Strict and Genetic Identity: An Illustration of the Relations of Logic to Metaphysics." *Structure, Method, and Meaning: Essays in Honor of Henry M. Sheffer*, eds. Horace M. Kallen et al. (New York: Liberal Arts P, 1951): 242-54.

146. "Philosophy of Religion in the United States." *Philosophy and Phenomenological Research* 11, 3 (1951): 406-10. French translation, "La Philosophie de la religion aux Etats-Unis," in *Les Etudes Philosophiques* 7, 1-2 (1952): 50-56.

147. Discussion: "Arthur Berndtson on Mystical Experience." *Personalist* 32, 2 (1951): 191-93.

148. Review of Kelvin Van Nuys. *Science and Cosmic Purpose* (New York: Harper, 1949). *Review of Religion* 16, 1-2 (1951): 79-84.

149. "The Relativity of Nonrelativity: Some Reflections on Firstness." *Studies in the Philosophy of Charles Sanders Peirce*, eds. Philip P. Wiener and Frederic H. Young (Cambridge: Harvard UP, 1952): 215-24.

150. "Radhakrishnan on Mind, Matter, and God." *The Philosophy of Saevepalli Radhakrishnan*, ed. Paul Arthur Schilpp. The Library of Living Philosophers, Vol. 8. (New York: Tudor, 1952): 315-22.

151. "Tillich's Doctrine of God." *The Theology of Paul Tillich*. The Library of Living Theology, Vol. 1, eds. Charles W. Kegley and Robert W. Bretall (New York: Macmillan, 1952): 164-95.

152. "Time, Death, and Eternal Life." *Journal of Religion* 32, 2 (1952): 97-107.

Reprinted in *Classical and Contemporary Readings in the Philosophy of Religion*. 2nd ed. John Hick (Englewood Cliffs, New Jersey: Prentice-Hall, 1970): 357-69.

Incorporated into chapter 10 of *Logic of Perfection*.

153. Review of Georg Siegmund. *Naturordnung als Quelle der Gotteserkenntnis: Neubegründung des theologischen Gottesbeweises* (Freiburg: Herder, 1950). *Philosophy and Phenomenological Research* 12, 4 (1952): 584-85.

154. "Politics and the Metaphysics of Freedom." *Enquête sur la liberté, Fédération internationale des sociétés de philosophie.* Publié avec le concours de l'u.n.e.s.c.o (Paris: Hermann, 1953): 79-85.

155. "Noch einmal, das Wissen Gottes." *Philosophisches Jahrbuch* 62, 2 (Freiburg-München: Verlag Karl Alber, 1953): 409-11.

156. "Spirit as Life Freely Participating in Life." *Biosophical Review* 10, 2 (1953): 31-32.

157. "The Monistic Theory of Expression." *Journal of Philosophy* 50, 14 (1953): 425-34.

158. Review of John Wisdom. *Philosophy and Psycho-Analysis* (New York: Philosophical Library, 1953). *Ethics* 63, 4 (1953): 317-18.

159. Discussion: "The Immortality of the Past: Critique of a Prevalent Misinterpretation." *Review of Metaphysics* 7, 1 (1953): 98-112.

160. Symposium: "Are Religious Dogmas Cognitive and Meaningful?" *Journal of Philosophy* 51, 5 (1954): 148-50.

161. Review of Risieri Frondizi. *The Nature of the Self* (New Haven: Yale UP, 1953). *Philosophy and Phenomenological Research* 14, 3 (1954): 419-20.

162. "The Kinds of Theism: A Reply [to Taubes]." *Journal of Religion* 34, 2 (1954): 127-31.

163. "Mind, Matter, and Freedom." *Scientific Monthly* 78, 5 (1954): 314-20. Chapter 8 of *Logic of Perfection*.

164. Review Article: "Whitehead's Philosophy of Reality as Socially-Structured Process" (apropos *Alfred North Whitehead: An Anthology*, selected by F.S.C. Northrop and Mason Gross [New York: Macmillan, 1953]). *Chicago Review* 8, 2 (1954): 60-77. Chapter 7 of *Whitehead's Philosophy*.

165. Review of F. W. Eggleston. *Reflections of an Australian Liberal* (Melbourne: Cheshire, 1953). *Ethics* 64, 4 (1954): 332.

166. "Biology and the Spiritual view of the World: A Comment on Dr. Birch's Paper." *Christian Scholar* 37, 3 (1954): 408-09.

167. "Russian Metaphysics: Some Reactions to Zenkovsky's History." *Review of Metaphysics* 8, 1 (1954): 61-78. Incorporated into chapter 11 of *Logic of Perfection*.

168. "Causal Necessities: An Alternative to Hume." *Philosophical Review* 63, 4 (1954): 479-99.

169. Review of J. Defever, S. J. *La Preuve réelle de Dieu* (Paris: Desclée de Brouwer, 1953). *Philosophy and Phenomenological Research* 15, 2 (1954): 285-86.

170. Review of Brand Blanshard. *The Nature of Thought* (London: Allen and Unwin, 1959). *Philosophische Rundschau* 3, 1-2 (1955): 119-20.

171. "Process as Inclusive Category: A Reply [to John E. Smith]." *Journal of Philosophy* 52, 4 (1955): 94-102.

172. Review of Eranos et al. *Spirit and Nature, Papers from the Eranos Yearbooks*, vol. 1. (New York: Pantheon, 1954). *Journal of Religion* 35, 2 (1955): 106-07.

173. Review of Wilmon Henry Sheldon. *God and Polarity* (New Haven: Yale UP, 1954). *Philosophical Review* 64, 2 (1955): 312-16. Chapter 15 of *Creativity in American Philosophy*.

174. Panel Discussion: 1955 Edward Gallahue Seminar in Religion and Psychology at the Menninger Foundation. *Passim.* [Mimeographed.]

175. "Some Empty Though Important Truths: A Preface to Metaphysics." *Review of Metaphysics* 8, 4 (1955): 553-68. Reprinted in *American Philosophers at Work: The Philosophic Scene in the United States*, ed. Sidney Hook (New York: Criterion Books, 1956): 225-35. Chapter 12 of *Logic of Perfection*.

176. "The Unity of Man and the Unity of Nature." *Emory University Quarterly* 11, 3 (1955): 129-41. Chapter 13 of *Logic of Perfection*.

177. "Royce's Mistake and Achievement." *Journal of Philosophy* 53, 3 (1956): 123-30. Chapter 6 of *Creativity in American Philosophy*.

178. Panel Discussion: 1956 Edward Gallahue Seminar in Religion and Psychology at the Menninger Foundation. *Passim.* [Mimeographed.]

179. "The Idea of Creation." (Colloquium No. 8). *Review of Metaphysics* 9, 3 (1956): 464-65.

180. Review of Robert Leet Patterson. *Irrationalism and Rationalism in Religion* (Durham: Duke UP, 1954). *Review of Religion* 20, 3-4 (1956): 211-13.

181. "The Idea of God—Literal or Analogical?" *Christian Scholar* 29, 2 (1956): 131-36. Chapter 3 of *Logic of Perfection*.

182. Discussion: "New Propositions and New Truths." *Review of Metaphysics* 9, 4 (1956): 656-61.

183. "Two Strata of Meaning in Religious Discourse." *Symposium on Philosophy of Religion, Southern Philosopher* 5, 3 (1956): 4-7. Expanded in *Logic of Perfection* as chapter 4, "Three Strata of Meaning of Religious Discourse." [cf. item 282].

184. "Some Reflections Suggested by H. Wolfson's *Philosophy of the Church Fathers, Vol. I: Faith, Trinity, Incarnation*." (Cambridge: Harvard UP, 1956). *Collection of Reviews*, Southern Society for Philosophy of Religion, J. R. Cresswell, Bibliographer (1957): 1-10. [Mimeographed]

185. "Whitehead and Berdyaev: Is there Tragedy in God?" *Journal of Religion* 37, 2 (1957): 71-84. Chapter 13 of *Whitehead's Philosophy*.

186. Review of William Ernest Hocking. *The Coming World Civilization* (New York: Harper, 1956). *Chicago Theological Seminary Register* 47, 5 (1957): 21-22. Also published in *Philosophy and Phenomenological Research* 17, 4 (1957): 562-63.

187. Review of Gerda Walter. *Ph̦nomenologie der Mystik* (Olten und Freiburg im Breisgau: Walter-Verlag, 1955). *Philosophy and Phenomenological Research* 18, 1 (1957): 140-41.

188. "Charles Peirce, Philosopher-Scientist." Charles Sanders Peirce Symposium, No.1. *Journal of Public Law* 7, 1 (1958): 2-12.

189. "Whitehead on Process: A Reply to Professor Eslick." *Philosophy and Phenomenological Research* 18, 4 (1958): 514-20.

190. "Science, Insecurity, and the Abiding Treasure." *Journal of Religion* 38, 3 (1958): 168-74. Abridged version in *The Spirit of American Philosophy: An Anthology*, selected, edited, and introduced by Gerald E. Myers (New York: Capricorn Books,

1971): 327-32. Incorporated into chapter 9 of *Logic of Perfection.*

191. "Outlines of a Philosophy of Nature, Part I." *Personalist* 39, 3 (1958): 239-48. "Outlines of a Philosophy of Nature, Part II." *Personalist* 39, 4 (1958): 380-91.

192. "Freedom Requires Indeterminism and Universal Causality." *Journal of Philosophy* 55, 19 (1958): 793-811. Chapter 6 of *Logic of Perfection.*

193. "Metaphysical Statements as Nonrestrictive and Existential." *Review of Metaphysics* 12, 1 (1958): 35-47. Chapter 8 of *Creative Synthesis.*

194. "The Logical Structure of Givenness." *Philosophical Quarterly* [Scotland] 8, 33 (1958): 307-16.

195. "The Philosophy of Creative Synthesis." *Journal of Philosophy* 55, 22 (1958): 944-53. Reprinted in *Americana: A Monthly Journal of Humanities, Social Sciences, and Natural Sciences* [Tokyo] 5, 8 (1959): 80-90. Tokyo, U.S.I.S. In Japanese. EC 1968. Part of chapter 1 of *Creative Synthesis.* [cf. items 220, 221, and 415]

196. Discussion: "The Structure of Metaphysics: A Criticism of Lazerowitz's Theory." *Philosophy and Phenomenological Research* 19, 2 (1958): 226-40. Incorporated into chapter 5 of *Wisdom as Moderation.*

197. "Four Unrefuted Forms of the Ontological Argument." *Journal of Philosophical Studies* [Kyoto, Japan] 40, 1 (1959): 1-15. In Japanese, with English Summary.

198. "A Philosopher's Assessment of Christianity." *Religion and Culture: Essays in Honor of Paul Tillich,* ed. Walter Leibrecht (New York: Harper, 1959): 167-80.

199. "John Wisdom On 'Gods': Two Views of the Logic of Theism." *Downside Review* [Bath, England] (1958-1959): 5-17. Chapter 5 of *Logic of Perfection.*

200. "The Principle of Shared Creativity." *Unitarian Symposia No. 6, What Can Religion Offer Modern Man?* (1959): 1-8.

201. "Freedom, Individuality, and Beauty in Nature." *Snowy Egret* 24, 2 (1960): 5-14. [Mimeographed]

202. "Equalitarianism and the Great Inequalities." *Emory Alumnus* 36, 7 (1960): 24-25, 49.

203. "Jinsei no mokuteki" ("The Aim of Life.") Trans. Toshio Mikoda, *Tetsugaku Kenkyu* [Journal of Philosophical Studies, Japan] 41, 2 (1960): 1-13.

204. "The Buddhist-Whiteheadian View of the Self and the Religious Traditions." *Proceedings of the Ninth International Congress for the History of Religions* (Tokyo and Kyoto: Maruzen, 1960 [1958]): 298-302.

205. "Whitehead and Contemporary Philosophy." *The Relevance of Whitehead: Philosophical Essays in Commemoration of the Centenary of the Birth of Alfred North Whitehead,* ed. Ivor Leclerc (London: Allen and Unwin, 1961): 21-43. Chapter 10 of *Whitehead's Philosophy.*

206. "Metaphysics and the Modality of Existential Judgments." *The Relevance of Whitehead: Philosophical Essays in Commemoration of the Centenary of the Birth of Alfred North Whitehead,* ed. Ivor Leclerc (London: Allen and Unwin, 1961): 107-21.

207. "Hume's Metaphysics and Its Present-Day Influence." *New Scholasticism* 35, 2 (1961): 152-71. Chapter 13 of *Insights and Oversights.*

208. "The Social Structure of Experience." *Philosophy* 36, 137 (1961): 97-111.

209. "The Structure of Givenness." *Philosophical Forum* 18 (1960-1961): 22-39. Chapter 16 of *Creativity in American Philosophy*. Reprinted as Appendix 2 of *Hartshorne and Brightman on God*.

210. "God's Existence: A Conceptual Problem." *Religious Experience and Truth: A Symposium*, ed. Sidney Hook (New York UP, 1961): 211-19.

211. Discussion: "Professor Hall on Perception." *Philosophy and Phenomenological Research* 21, 4 (1961): 563-71.

212. "Tillich and the Other Great Tradition." *Anglican Theological Review* 43, 3 (1961): 245-59. Part of chapter 7 in *Creative Synthesis*.

213. "The Logic of the Ontological Argument." *Journal of Philosophy* 58, 17 (1961): 471-73.

214. Discussion: "Absolute Objects and Relative Subjects: A Reply [to F. H. Parker]." *Review of Metaphysics* 15, 1 (1961): 174-88.

215. "Man in Nature." *Experience, Existence, and the Good: Essays in Honor of Paul Weiss*, ed. Irwin C. Lieb (Carbondale: Southern Illinois UP, 1961): 89-99.

216. "Whitehead, the Anglo-American Philosopher-Scientist." *Proceedings of the American Catholic Philosophical Association* (Washington: Catholic U of America, 1961): 163-71. Chapter 9 of *Whitehead's Philosophy*.

217. Introduction to Second Edition, *Saint Anselm: Basic Writings*. Trans. S. W. Deane (La Salle, Illinois: Open Court Publishing Company, 1962): 1-19.

218. "The Modern World and a Modern View of God." *Crane Review* 4, 2 (1962): 73-85. Also in *Philosophy of Religion: Contemporary Perspectives*, ed. Norbert O. Schedler (New York: Macmillan Publishing Co., Inc., 1974): 469-79.

219. "What Did Anselm Discover?" *Union Seminary Quarterly Review* 17, 3 (1962): 213-222. An expanded version published in *The Many-Faced Argument*, eds. John Hick and Arthur C. McGill (New York: Macmillan, 1967): 321-33. The 1962 version of the paper is reprinted as chapter 8 of *Insights and Oversights*.

220. "La Creatividad Participada." Trans. Sira Jaén. *Revista de Filosofía de la Universidad de Costa Rica* 3, 11 (1962): 237-44. Spanish version of most of chapter 1 of *Creative Synthesis*. [cf. items 195, 221, and 415]

221. "Religion and Creative Experience." *Darshana, an International Quarterly of Philosophy, Psychology, Psychical Research, Religion, Mysticism, and Sociology* [India] 2, 1 (1962): 47-52. Also in *Unitarian Register and Universalist Leader* 141, 6 (1962): 9-11. Part of Chapter 1 of *Creative Synthesis*. [cf. items 195, 220, and 415]

222. "Mind as Memory and Creative Love." *Theories of the Mind*, ed. Jordan M. Scher (New York: The Free Press of Glencoe, 1962): 440-63.

223. Discussion: "How Some Speak and Yet Do Not Speak of God." *Philosophy and Phenomenological Research* 23, 2 (1962): 274-76. Part of chapter 5 of *Wisdom as Moderation*.

224. "Individual Differences and the Ideal of Equality." *New South* 18, 2 (1963): 3-8. Chapter 14 of *Zero Fallacy*.

225. "Alternative Conceptions of God." *Religious Belief and Philosophical Thought*. ed. William P. Alston (New York: Harcourt, Brace, & World, 1963): 320-

37. Reprinted from *Man's Vision of God*.

226. "Further Fascination of the Ontological Argument: Replies to Richardson." *Union Seminary Quarterly Review* 18, 3 [Part I] (1963): 244-45.

227. "Whitehead's Novel Intuition." *Alfred North Whitehead: Essays On His Philosophy*, ed. George L. Kline (Englewood Cliffs, New Jersey: Prentice-Hall, 1963): 18-26. Chapter 11 of *Whitehead's Philosophy*.

228. "Sensation in Psychology and Philosophy." *Southern Journal of Philosophy* 1, 2 (1963): 3-14.

229. "Rationale of the Ontological Proof." *Theology Today* 20, 2 (1963): 278-83.

230. "Whitehead's Conception of God" and "Whitehead's Theory of Prehension." In *Actas: Segundo Congreso Extraordinario Inter-americano de Filosofía, 22-26 Julio, 1961* (San José, Costa Rica: Imprenta Nacional, 1963 [misprinted 1962]): 163-170.

231. Communication: "Finite or Finite-Infinite?" *Philosophy and Phenomenological Research* 24, 1 (1963): 149.

232. "Real Possibility." *Journal of Philosophy* 60, 21 (1963): 593-605.

233. "Present Prospects for Metaphysics." *The Monist* 47, 2 (1963): 188-210. Reprinted in *Process Philosophy: Basic Writings*, eds. Jack R. Sibley and Pete A. Y. Gunter (Washington D.C.: UP of America, 1978): 199-212. Chapter 3 of *Creative Synthesis*.

234. "Man's Fragmentariness." *Wesleyan Studies in Religion* 41, 6 (1963-1964): 17-28. Chapter 6 of *Wisdom as Moderation*.

235. "Abstract and Concrete in God: A Reply [to Julian Hartt]." *Review of Metaphysics* 17, 2 (1963): 289-95.

236. "Santayana's Defiant Eclecticism." *Journal of Philosophy* 61, 1 (1964): 35-44. Reprinted in *Animal Faith and Spiritual Life*, ed. John Lachs (New York: Appleton-Century-Crofts, 1967): 33-43. Chapter 10 of *Creativity in American Philosophy*.

237. "Thinking About Thinking Machines." *Texas Quarterly* 7, 1 (1964): 131-40.

238. Discussion: "What the Ontological Proof Does Not Do." *Review of Metaphysics* 17, 4 (1964): 608-09.

239. "From Colonial Beginnings to Philosophical Greatness." *The Monist* 48, 3 (1964): 317-31. Chapter 1 of *Creativity in American Philosophy*.

240. Comments and Criticism: "Deliberation and Excluded Middle." *Journal of Philosophy* 61, 16 (1964): 476-77.

241. Replies to "Interrogation of Charles Hartshorne, conducted by William Alston."

Philosophical Interrogations, eds. Sydney and Beatrice Rome (New York: Holt, Rinehart, and Winston, 1964): 321-54. Questions to: John Wild, 158-160; Brand Blanshard, 205; Paul Tillich, 374-375.

242. "Is God's Existence a State of Affairs?" *Faith and the Philosophers*, ed. John Hick (New York: St. Martin's Press, 1964): 26-33.

243. "El valor como disfrute del contraste y la teoría acumulativa del proceso." Trans. J. L. González, *Dianoia, Annuario de Filosofía* 10 (1964): 182-194.

244. "Charles Peirce's 'One Contribution to Philosophy' and His Most Serious Mistake." *Studies in the Philosophy of Charles Sanders Peirce. Second Series*, eds. Edward G. Moore and Richard S. Robin (Amherst: U of Massachusetts P, 1964): 455-74.

245. "Negative Facts and the Analogical Inference to 'Other Mind'." *Dr. S. Radhakrishan Souvenir Volume*, eds. Prof. J. P. Atreya et al. (Moradabad [India]: Darshana International, 1964): 147-52.

246. "The Idea of a Worshipful Being." *Southern Journal of Philosophy* 2, 4 (1964): 165-67.

247. "God as the Supreme Relativity." *Japanese Religions* 4, 1 (1964): 30-33.

248. "The Necessarily Existent." *The Ontological Argument*, ed. Alvin Plantinga (New York: Anchor Books, Doubleday, 1965): 123-35. Reprinted in *Philosophy of Religion*, eds. George L. Abernethy and Thomas A. Langford, 2nd ed. (New York: Macmillan, 1968): 238-47. Chapter 9 of *Man's Vision of God*.

249. "The Meaning of 'Is Going to Be'." *Mind* 74, 293 (1965): 46-58.

250. "The Theistic Proofs." *Union Seminary Quarterly Review* 20, 2 (1965): 115-29. Chapter 2 of *Natural Theology*.

251. "Abstract and Concrete Approaches to Deity." *Union Seminary Quarterly Review* 20, 3 (1965): 265-70.

252. "A Metaphysics of Individualism." *Innocence and Power: Individualism in Twentieth-Century America*, ed. Gordon Mills (Austin: U of Texas P, 1965): 131-46.

253. "Determinism, Memory, and the Metaphysics of Becoming." *Pacific Philosophy Forum* 4, 4 (1965): 81-85.

254. "The Social Theory of Feelings." *Southern Journal of Philosophy* 3, 2 (1965): 87-93. Reprinted in *Persons, Privacy, and Feeling: Essays in the Philosophy of Mind*, ed. Dwight Van de Vate, Jr. (Memphis: Memphis State UP, 1970): 39-51.

255. "The Development of Process Philosophy." Introduction to *Philosophers of Process*, ed. Douglas Browning (New York: Random House, 1965): v-xii. Also published in *Process Theology: Basic Writings*, ed. Ewert H. Cousins (New York: Newman P, 1971): 47-64.

256. "Religious Aspects of Necessity and Contingency." *Great Issues Concerning Theism*, ed. Charles H. Manson, Jr. (Salt Lake City: U of Utah P, 1965): 147-64. Reprinted in *And More About God*, eds. Lewis M. Rogers and Charles H. Monson, Jr. (Salt Lake City: U of Utah P, 1969): 145-61.

257. "Criteria for Ideas of God." *Rice University Studies* 51, 4 (1965): 85-95. Also in *Insight and Vision: Essays in Philosophy in Honor of Radoslav Andrea Tsanoff*, ed. Konstantin Kolenda (San Antonio: Principia P of Trinity University, 1966): 85-95.

258. "Comment." *The Creative Advance*, by Eugene H. Peters (St. Louis: Bethany P, 1966): 133-43.

259. "The Two Possible Philosophical Definitions of God." In *Actas: XIII Congreso Internacional de Filosofía*, volumen 9 (Mexico City: Universidad Nacional Autonoma de Mexico, 1966): 121.

260. "A New Look at the Problem of Evil." *Current Philosophical Issues: Essays in Honor of Curt John Ducasse*, ed. Frederick C. Dommeyer (Springfield, Illinois: Charles C. Thomas, 1966): 201-12.

261. "Idealism and Our Experience of Nature." *Philosophy, Religion, and the*

Coming World Civilization: Essays in Honor of William Ernest Hocking, ed. Leroy S. Rouner (The Hague: Martinus Nijhoff, 1966): 70-80. Chapter 12 of *Creativity in American Philosophy*.

262. "Tillich and the Non-theological Meaning of Theological Terms." *Religion in Life* 35, 5 (1966): 674-85. Reprinted in *Paul Tillich: Retrospect and Future* [pamphlet]. (Nashville: Abingdon P, 1966): 19-30.

263. "Some Reflections on Metaphysics and Language." *Foundations of Language: International Journal of Language and Philosophy* 2, 1 (1966): 20-32.

264. "Is the Denial of Existence Ever Contradictory?" *Journal of Philosophy* 63, 4 (1966): 85-93. Author's abstract in *The Review of Metaphysics* 19, 4 (1966): 836.

265. "The Idea of Creativity in American Philosophy." *Journal of Kamatak University* [India]: *Social Sciences II* (1966): 1-13.

266. Review of N. S. Srivastava. *Contemporary Indian Philosophy* (Delhi: M.R.M. Lal, 1965). *Research Journal of Philosophy* (Ranchi University [India]) 1, 1 (1966): 110-11.

267. "Religion in Process Philosophy." *Religion in Philosophical and Cultural Perspective*, eds. J. Clayton Feaver and William Horosz (Princeton, New Jersey: D. Van Nostrand Co, 1967): 246-58.

268. "Royce and the Collapse of Idealism." *Revue internationale de philosophie* 23, 79-80 (1967, Fasc. 1-2): 46-59.

269. "Kagaku, Geijyutsu, Shukyo-Kofuku no Gensen to shite no." ("Science, Art, and Religion as Sources of Happiness.") Trans. Matao Noda. *Japan-American Forum* 13, 3 (1967): 47-66.

270. "God and the Social Structure of Reality," "The Significance of Man in the Life of God," and Answers to Questions. *Theology in Crisis: A Colloquium on 'The Credibility of God'* (New Concord, Ohio: Muskingum College, 1967): 19-32, 40-43, 44-50.

271. "Pantheism." *Encyclopedia Britannica*, Vol. 17 (1967): 233-34.

272. "Psychology and the Unity of Knowledge." *Southern Journal of Philosophy* 5, 2 (1967): 81-90.

273. "The Dipolar Conception of Deity." *Review of Metaphysics* 21, 2 (1967): 273-89.

274. "Necessity." *Review of Metaphysics* 21, 2 (1967): 290-96.

275. "Rejoinder to Purtill." *Review of Metaphysics* 21, 2 (1967): 308-09.

276. "Martin Buber's Metaphysics." *The Philosophy of Martin Buber*, eds. Paul Arthur Schilpp and Maurice Friedman. The Library of Living Philosophers, Vol. 12 (La Salle, Illinois: Open Court, 1967): 49-68. Also published as "Martin Buber's Metaphysik" in *Martin Buber*, herausgegeben von Schilpp u. Friedman (Stuttgart: Kohlhammer Verlag, 1963): 42-61.

277. "What Metaphysics Is." *Journal of Kamatak University: Social Sciences III* (1967): 1-15. Chapter 2 of *Creative Synthesis*; Chapter 6 of *Zero Fallacy*.

278. "The Irreducibly Modal Structure of the Argument." *The Many-Faced Argument*, eds. John Hick and Arthur C. McGill (New York: Macmillan, 1967): 334-40. Reprinted from chapter 2, part VI of *Logic of Perfection*.

279. "Process Philosophy as a Resource for Christian Thought." *Philosophical*

Resources for Christian Thought, ed. Perry LeFevre (Nashville: Abingdon P, 1968): 44-66.

280. "The Divine Relativity." *Philosophy of Religion*, eds. George L. Abernethy and Thomas A. Langford. 2nd ed. (New York: Macmillan, 1968): 321-29. From *Divine Relativity*.

281. "Order and Chaos." *The Concept of Order*, ed. Paul G. Kuntz (Seattle: U of Washington P, 1968): 253-67.

282. "Three Strata of Meaning in Religious Discourse." *Philosophy and Religion: Some Contemporary Perspectives*, ed. Jerry H. Gill (Minneapolis: Burgess, 1968): 173-82. Chapter 4 of *Logic of Perfection*. [cf. item 183].

283. "The Aesthetics of Birdsong." *Journal of Aesthetics and Art Criticism* 26, 3 (1968): 311-15.

284. "Kant's Refutation Still Not Convincing: A Reply [to W. H. Baumer]." *The Monist* 52, 2 (1968): 312-16.

285. "Lewis's Treatment of Memory." *The Philosophy of C. I. Lewis*, ed. Paul Arthur Schilpp. The Library of Living Philosophers, Vol. 13 (La Salle, Illinois: Open Court, 1968): 395-414. Chapter 13 of *Creativity in American Philosophy*.

286. "Armchair and Laboratory: A Philosopher Looks at Psychology." *Newsletter, Division 24 of the American Psychological Association* 2, 3 (1968): 1-4.

287. "Born Equal: The Importance and Limitations of an Ideal." *Parables and Problems* (Winona, Minnesota: College of St. Teresa, 1968): 59-71. [Mimeographed]

288. "The Case for Idealism." *Philosophical Forum* 1, 1 (1968): 7-23.

289. "The God of Religion and the God of Philosophy." *Talk of God: Royal Institute of Philosophy Lectures, Vol. Two 1967-1968* (London: Macmillan, 1969): 152-67. Originally Broadcast Monday, June 10, 1968, BBC London Third Programme, *The Listener*.

290. "Duality versus Dualism and Monism." *Japanese Religions* 5, 1 (1969): 51-63.

291. "Leibniz und das Geheimnis der Materie." *Studia Leibnitiana: Akten des Internationalen Leibniz-Kongresses, Hannover, 14-19 November 1966, Band II: Mathematik-Naturwissenschaften* (Wiesbaden: Franz Steiner Verlag GMBH, 1969): 166-75.

292. "Whitehead in French Perspective: A Review Article." [Review of Alix Parmentier, *La Philosophie de Whitehead et le problème de Dieu* (Paris: Beauchesne, 1968)]. *Thomist* 33, 3 (1969): 573-81.

293. Response to *Directives from Charles Hartshorne and Henry Nelson Wieman Critically Analyzed: Philosophy of Creativity Monograph Series*, Vol. 1, ed. William S. Minor (Carbondale: The Foundation for Creative Philosophy, Inc., 1969): 33-42.

294. "Divine Absoluteness and Divine Relativity." *Transcendence*, eds. Herbert W. Richardson and Donald R. Cutler (Boston: Beacon P, 1969): 164-71.

295. "Metaphysics in North America." *Contemporary Philosophy: A Survey*, ed. Raymond Klibansky (Florence: La Nuova Italia Editrice, 1969): 36-49.

296. "Whitehead and Ordinary Language." *Southern Journal of Philosophy* 7, 4 (1969-1970): 437-45. Chapter 12 of *Whitehead's Philosophy*.

297. Preface of *Berdyaev's Philosophy of History*, ed. David Bonner Richardson (The Hague: Martinus Nihjoff, 1970): ix-xiii.

298. "Why Study Birds?" *Virginia Quarterly Review* 46, 1 (1970): 133-40.

299. "Recollections of Famous Philosophers and Other Important Persons." *Southern Journal of Philosophy* 8, 1 (1970): 67-82. Chapter 13 of *Darkness and Light.*

300. "Two Forms of Idolatry." *International Journal for Philosophy of Religion* 1, 1 (1970): 3-15.

301. "Six Theistic Proofs." *Monist* 54, 2 (1970): 159-80. Chapter 14 of *Creative Synthesis.*

302. "Equality, Freedom, and the Insufficiency of Empiricism." *Southern Journal of Philosophy* 1, 3 (1970): 20-27.

303. "Eternity," "Absolute," "God." *Prophetic Voices: Ideas and Words on Revolution*, ed. Ned O'Gorman (New York: Random House, 1969; New York: Vintage Books, 1970): 130-48.

304. "The Development of My Philosophy." *Contemporary American Philosophy: Second Series*, ed. John E. Smith (London: Allen & Unwin, 1970): 211-28.

305. "Ontological Primacy: A Reply to Buchler." *Journal of Philosophy* 67, 23 (1970): 979-86. Reprinted in *Explorations in Whitehead's Philosophy*, eds. Lewis S. Ford and George L. Kline (New York: Fordham UP, 1983): 295-303.

306. "Charles Hartshorne's Recollections of Editing the Peirce Papers." *Transactions of the Charles S. Peirce Society* 6, 3-4 (1970): 149-59.

307. "Deity as the Inclusive Transcendence." *Evolution in Perspective: Commentaries in Honor of Pierre Lecomte du Noüy*, eds. George N. Shuster and Ralph E. Thorson (Notre Dame and London: U of Notre Dame P, 1970): 155-60.

308. "The Formally Possible Doctrines of God." *Classical and Contemporary Readings in the Philosophy of Religion*, ed. John Hick. Second Edition. (Englewood Cliffs, New Jersey: Prentice-Hall, 1970): 336-57. Also printed in *Process Philosophy and Christian Thought*, eds. Delwin Brown, Ralph E. James, Jr., and Gene Reeves (Indianapolis: Bobbs-Merrill, 1971): 188-214. Chapter 1 of *Man's Vision of God.*

309. "Mind and Matter in Ryle, Ayer, and C. I. Lewis." *Idealistic Studies* 1, 1 (1971): 13-32. Chapter 24 of *Insights and Oversights.*

310. "Are There Absolutely Specific Universals?" *Journal of Philosophy* 68, 3 (1971): 76-78.

311. "Can Man Transcend His Animality?" *The Monist* 55, 2 (1971): 208-217. Chapter 7 of *Wisdom as Moderation.*

312. "Selfishness in Man." *PHP* [Peace Happiness Prosperity] 1, 8 (1971): 24-25.

313. "Could There Have Been Nothing? A Reply [to Houston Craighead]." *Process Studies* 1, 1 (1971): 25-28.

314. "Expression and Association." *Artistic Expression*, ed. John Hospers (New York: Appleton-Century-Crofts, 1971): 204-17. Chapter 5, Section 23 of *Philosophy and Psychology of Sensation.*

315. "Obligability and Determinism." *Journal of Social Philosophy* 2, 2 (1971): 1-2. Reprinted in *Philosophy for a Changing Society*, ed. Creighton Peden

(Reynoldsburg, Ohio: Advocate Publishing Co., 1982): 95-96.

316. "Philosophical and Religious Uses of 'God'." *Process Theology: Basic Writings*, ed. Ewert H. Cousins (New York: Newman P, 1971): 101-18. Chapter 1 of *Natural Theology*.

317. "Can There Be Proofs for the Existence of God?" *Religious Language and Knowledge*, eds. Robert H. Ayers and William T. Blackstone (Athens: U of Georgia P, 1972): 62-75.

318. "Mortimer Adler as Philosopher: A Criticism and Appreciation." *American Scholar* 41, 2 (1972): 269-74. Chapter 19 of *Creativity in American Philosophy*.

319. "A Conversation with Charles Hartshorne at Hiram College." Edited by Eugene Peters. *Eclectic: A Journal of Ideas* 1, 1 (1972): 1-18.

320. Review of Paul Ramsay. *Fabricated Man* (New Haven: Yale UP, 1970). *Philosophy Forum* 12, 1 & 2 (1972): 149-52.

321. Review of Paul Weiss. *The God We Seek* (Carbondale: Southern Illinois P, 1964). *Review of Metaphysics* 25 [supplement] (1972): 108-16. Chapter 19 of *Creativity in American Philosophy*.

322. "Personal Identity from A to Z." *Process Studies* 2, 3 (1972): 209-15.

323. Feature Book Review: "Some Thoughts Suggested by [Irwin C.] Lieb's *Four Faces of Man*." (Philadelphia: U of Pennsylvania P, 1971). *International Philosophical Quarterly* 13, 1 (1973): 131-34.

324. "Some Thoughts on 'Souls' and Neighborly Love." *Anglican Theological Review* 55, 2 (1973): 144-47.

325. "Analysis and Cultural Lag in Philosophy." *Southern Journal of Philosophy* 11, 2-3 (1973): 105-12.

326. "Being and Becoming: Review of Harold N. Lee. *Percepts, Concepts, and Theoretic Knowledge*." *Review of Books and Religion* 2, 9 (1973): 7.

327. "Process and the Nature of God." *Traces of God in a Secular Culture*, ed. George F. McLean, O.M.I (New York: Alba House, 1973): 117-41.

328. "Creativity and the Deductive Logic of Causality." *Review of Metaphysics* 27, 1 (1973): 62-74.

329. "Pensées sur ma vie," 26-32; "Thoughts on my Life," 60-66. *Bilingual Journal, Lecomte du Noüy Association* 5 (1973).

330. "Charles Peirce and Quantum Mechanics." *Transactions of the Charles S. Peirce Society* 9, 4 (1973): 191-201. See also *Abstracts of Communications Sent to the XVth World Congress of Philosophy*. Varna, Sept. 17-22, 1973. Bulgarian Organizing Committee, International Federation of Philosophical Societies.

331. "Husserl and Whitehead on the Concrete." *Phenomenology: Continuation and Criticism—Essays in Memory of Dorion Cairns*, eds. F. Kersten and R. Zaner (The Hague: Martinus Nijhoff, 1973): 90-104. Chapter 23 of *Insights and Oversights*.

332. "Ideas and Theses of Process Philosophers." *Two Process Philosophers: Hartshorne's Encounter with Whitehead*. AAR Studies in Religion Number Five (Tallahassee, Florida: American Academy of Religion, 1973): 100-03.

333. "Science and Quality." *Sound Seminars: Tapes in Philosophy*. New York: McGraw-Hill, 1954, 1973.

334. "Contribuciones Permanentes de Spinoza." [Spanish translation of

"Spinoza's Permanent Contributions."] *Folia humanistica: ciencias, artes, letras* 12 (1974): 121-29.

335. "Twelve Elements of My Philosophy." *Southwestern Journal of Philosophy* 5, 1 (1974): 7-15.

336. Abstract: "Do Philosophers Know That They Have Bodies?" *Abstracts of Papers, 1974. Annual Conference of the Australasian Association of Philosophy* (Canberra: Australian National U, 1974): 7-8.

337. "Philosophy after Fifty Years." *Mid-Twentieth Century American Philosophy: Personal Statements*, ed. Peter A. Bertocci (New York: Humanities P, 1974): 140-54.

338. "The Environmental Results of Technology." *Philosophy and Environmental Crisis*, ed. William T. Blackstone (Athens: U of Georgia P, 1974): 69-78.

339. "Beyond Enlightened Self-Interest: A Metaphysics of Ethics." *Ethics* 84, 3 (1974): 201-16. Reprinted in *Religious Experience and Process Theology*, eds. Harry James Cargas and Bernard Lee (New York: Paulist P, 1976): 301-322. Also published in *Process Philosophy: Basic Writings*, eds. Jack R. Sibley and Pete A. Y. Gunter (Washington, D.C.: UP of America, 1978): 395-416. Chapter 12 of *Zero Fallacy*.

340. "Perception and the Concrete Abstractness of Science." *Philosophy and Phenomenological Research* 34, 4 (1974): 465-76. Chapter 9 of *Zero Fallacy*.

341. "The Nature of Philosophy." *Philosophy in Context: An Experiment in Teaching*, Vol. 4, ed. Leslie Armour (Cleveland State UP, 1975): 7-16.

342. "Love and Dual Transcendence." *Union Seminary Quarterly Review* 30, 2-4 (1975): 94-100.

343. "Whitehead's Differences from Buddhism." *Philosophy East and West* 25, 4 (1975): 407-13.

344. "Whitehead and Leibniz: A Comparison." *Contemporary Studies in Philosophical Idealism*, eds. John Howie and Thomas O. Buford (Cape Cod, Massachusetts: Claude Starke, 1975): 95-115.

345. "Do Birds Enjoy Singing? (An Ornitho-Philosophical Discourse)." *Bulletin of the Texas Ornithological Society* 8 (1975): 2-5. Chapter 2 of *Zero Fallacy*.

346. "The Centrality of Reason in Philosophy (Replies to Questions for Charles Hartshorne)." *Philosophy in Context*, Supplement to Volume 4 (1975): 5-11.

347. Discussion: "Synthesis as Polyadic Inclusion: A Reply to Sessions." *Southern Journal of Philosophy* 14, 2 (1976): 245-55.

348. "Mysticism and Rationalistic Metaphysics." *The Monist* 59, 4 (1976): 463-69. Also published in *Understanding Mysticism*, ed. Richard Woods (Garden City, New York: Image, 1980): 415-21.

349. "Psychicalism and the Leibnizian Principle." *Studia Leibnitiana* 8, 2 (1976): 154-59. Chapter 8 of *Zero Fallacy*.

350. "Why Psychicalism? Comments on Keeling's and Shepherd's Criticisms." *Process Studies* 6, 1 (1976): 67-72.

351. "Additional Reflections." [On Jean-Marie Breuvart's *Les Directives de la Symbolisation et les Modeles de Référence dans la Philosophie d'A. N. Whitehead*]. *Process Studies* 7, 4 (1977): 271-74.

352. "Bell's Theorem and Stapp's Revised View of Space-time." *Process Studies* 7, 3 (1977): 183-91.

353. "The Books That Shape Lives: Book Choices of Charles Hartshorne." *Christian Century* 44, 30 (1977): 860.

354. "Cobb's Theology of Ecology." *John Cobb's Theology in Process*, eds. David Ray Griffin and Thomas J. J. Altizer (Philadelphia: Westminster P, 1977): 112-15.

355. "The Duty to Happiness." *Catalyst Tape Talk* 9, 5 (1977): 4.

356. "John Hick on Logical and Ontological Necessity." *Religious Studies* 13, 2 (1977): 155-65.

357. "The Neglect of Relative Predicates in Modern Philosophy." *American Philosophical Quarterly* 14, 4 (1977): 309-18. Chapter 14 of *Insights and Oversights*.

358. "Physics and Psychics: The Place of Mind in Nature." *Mind in Nature: Essays on the Interface of Science and Philosophy*, eds. John B. Cobb, Jr. and David Ray Griffin (Washington, D.C.: UP of America, 1977): 89-96; also in this volume, "Response to Arthur Koestler's 'Free Will in a Hierarchic Context'," 66 and "Response to Bernhard Rensch's 'Arguments for Panpsychistic Identism'," 78.

359. "Whitehead's Metaphysical System." Trans. Schubert M. Ogden (from "Das metaphysische System Whiteheads"). *A Rational Faith: Essays in Honor of Rabbi Levi A. Olan*, ed. Jack Bemporad (New York: KTAV Publishing House, Inc., 1977): 107-123. German original in *Zeitschrift fur philosophische Forschung* 3, 4 (1949): 566-575. German version also in *Whitehead: Einführung in seine Kosmologie*. Beitr٫ge von Gernot Bohme, Charles Hartshorne, u.s.w. Herausgegeben von Ernest Wolf-Gazo (Freiburg/München: Verlag Karl Albers, 1980): 28-44.

360. "The Acceptance of Death." *Philosophical Aspects of Thanatology*, Vol. 1. eds. Florence M. Hetzler and Austin H. Kutscher (New York: MSS Information Corporation, 1978): 83-87.

361. "Can We Understand God?" *Louvain Studies* 7, 2 (1978): 75-84. Reprinted in *Framing a Vision of the World: Essays in Philosophy, Science and Religion*, eds. André Cloots and Santiago Sia (Leuven UP, 1999): 87-97.

362. Foreword to *The Ontological Argument of Charles Hartshorne* by George L. Goodwin (Missoula, MT: Scholars P, 1978): xi-xviii.

363. "Foundations for a Humane Ethics: What Human Beings Have in Common with Other Higher Animals." *On the Fifth Day: Animal Rights and Human Ethics*, eds. Richard K. Morris and Michael W. Fox (Washington, DC: Acropolis Books, 1978): 154-72.

364. "The Individual is a Society." *The Individual and Society: Essays Presented to David L. Miller on His Seventy-fifth Birthday*, eds. Michael P. Jones, Patricia O.F. Nobo, Jorge L. Nobo, and Yen-ling Chang. *Southwestern Journal of Philosophy* (1978): 73-88.

365. "A New World and a New World View." *The Life of Choice*, ed. Clark Kucheman (Boston: Beacon P, 1978): 82-92. (First given as a speech at University of Texas graduation convocation, 1976.)

366. "The Organism According to Process Philosophy." *Organism, Medicine, and Metaphysics: Essays in Honor of Hans Jones on his 75th Birthday, May 10th, 1978*, ed. Stuart Spicker (Dordrecht, Holland: D. Reidel, 1978): 137-54. Also in *Process in Context: Essays in Post-Whiteheadian Perspectives*, ed. Ernest Wolf-Gazo (New York:

Charles Hartshorne

Peter Lang Publishing, Inc., 1988): 69-92.

367. "Panpsychism: Mind as Sole Reality." *Ultimate Reality and Meaning* 1, 2 (1978): 115-29.

368. "A Philosophy of Death." *Philosophical Aspects of Thanatology*, Vol. 2. eds. Florence M. Hetzler and A. H. Kutscher (New York: MSS Information Corporation, 1978): 81-89.

369. Preface to *Process Philosophy: Basic Writings*, eds. Jack R. Sibley and Pete A. Y. Gunter (Washington D.C.: UP of America, 1978): 1-7.

370. "Reply to Eugene H. Peters." *Ultimate Reality and Meaning* 1, 3 (1978): 233-34.

371. "Theism in Asian and Western Thought." *Philosophy East and West* 28, 4 (1978): 401-11.

372. "The Mystery of Omnipotence is Too Deep for Human Reason." *The Power of God: Readings on Omnipotence and Evil*, eds. Linwood Urban and Douglas N. Walton (New York: Oxford UP, 1978): 249-251. Retitled excerpt from *Natural Theology*, 116-20.

373. "'Emptiness' and Fullness in Asiatic and Western Thought." *Journal of Chinese Philosophy* 6 (1979): 411-20.

374. "Charles Morris." *Semiotica* 28, 3-4 (1979): 193-94.

375. "God and Nature." *Anticipation* 25 (1979): 58-64.

376. "The Rights of the Subhuman World." *Environmental Ethics: An Interdisciplinary Journal Dedicated to the Philosophical Aspects of Environmental Problems* 1, 1 (1979): 49-60. German translation by Dr. Ilse Tödt: "Rechte nicht nur für die Menschen" published in *Zeitschrift für Evangelische Ethik* 22, 1 (1978): 3-14. English original published as chapter 9 of *Wisdom as Moderation*.

377. "Metaphysics Contributes to Ornithology." *Theoria to Theory* 13, 2 (1979): 127-40. Chapter 8 of *Wisdom as Moderation*.

378. "Whitehead's Revolutionary Concept of Prehension." *International Philosophical Quarterly* 19, 3 (1979): 253-63. Chapter 9 of *Creativity in American Philosophy*.

379. "Process Themes in Chinese Thought." *Journal of Chinese Philosophy* 6 (1979): 323-36.

380. Interview with Charles Hartshorne [conducted by Santiago Sia]. *Miltown Studies* 4 (1979): 1-23.

381. "Philosophy and Religion." *Program of the International Congress of Philosophy* on "Contemporary Problems of Philosophy and Religion" at Fu Jen Catholic University, Taipei, Taiwan (Dec. 28, 1979-Jan. 4, 1980): 26.

382. "James' Empirical Pragmatism." *American Journal of Theology and Philosophy* 1, 1 (1980): 14-20. Chapter 5 of *Creativity in American Philosophy*.

383. "My Neoclassical Metaphysics." *Tijdschrift voor Philosophie* 42, 1 (1980): 3-10.

384. "In Defense of Wordsworth's View of Nature." *Philosophy & Literature* 4, 1 (1980): 80-91.

385. Review of Karol Wojtyla. *The Acting Person* (Dordrecht: D. Reidel Publishing Co., 1979). *Philosophy and Phenomenological Research* 40, 3 (1980): 443-

153

44.

386. "Ethics and the Process of Living." *Man and His Conduct: Philosophical Essays in Honor of Risieri Frondizi*, ed. Jorge J. E. Gracia (Rio Piedras, Puerto Rico: Editorial Universitaria, 1980): 191-202.

387. "Pepper's Approach to Metaphysics." *Root Metaphor: The Live Thought of Stephen C. Pepper*. PAUNCH #53-54 (1980): 80-81.

388. "Understanding Freedom and Suffering." *Catalyst Tape Talk* 12, 9 (1980): 4-5 [cut and edited without consultation with author. Also, recorded tape available.]

389. "A Revision of Peirce's Categories." *The Monist* 63, 3 (1980): 277-89. Reprinted in *The Relevance of Charles Peirce*, ed. Eugene Freeman (La Salle, Illinois: Monist Library of Philosophy, 1983): 80-92. Chapter 7 of *Creativity in American Philosophy*.

390. "Understanding as Seeing to be Necessary." *The Philosophy of Brand Blanshard*, ed. Paul Arthur Schilpp. The Library of Living Philosophers, Vol. 15 (La Salle, Illinois: Open Court, 1980): 629-35.

391. "Response to Robert Neville's *Creativity and God*." *Process Studies* 10, 3-4 (1980): 93-97.

392. "A Conversation between Charles Hartshorne and Jan Van der Veken." *Louvain Studies* VII, 2 (1980): 129-42.

393. "Concerning Abortion: An Attempt at a Rational View." *The Christian Century* 98, 2 (1981): 42-45. Reprinted in *Speak Out Against the New Right*, ed. Herbert F. Vetter (Boston: Beacon P, 1982): 152-157. Also reprinted in *The Ethics of Abortion*, first edition, eds. Robert M. Baird and Stuart E. Rosenbaum (Buffalo, New York: Prometheus Books, 1989): 109-14.

394. "The Ethics of Contributionism." *Responsibilities to Future Generations: Environmental Ethics*, ed. Ernest Partridge (Buffalo: Prometheus P, 1981): 103-07.

395. "Critical Study: A Neglected Nonacademic Philosopher" [on Rudolf Jordan]. *Process Studies* 11, 3 (1981): 213-15.

396. "Neoclassical Metaphysics." *Philosophers on Their Own Work*, Vol. 8. Bern, Frankfurt, Las Vegas: Peter Lang, 1981): 63-104. In French and English.
Includes a list of publications.

397. "Science as the Search for the Hidden Beauty of the World." *The Aesthetic Dimension of Science* 1980 Nobel Conference, Number 16, ed. Deane W. Curtin (New York: Philosophical Library, 1982): 85-106. See also pp. 107, 108, 117, 119-120, 123-125, 128-129, 130, 131, 137, 140, 143.

398. "Creative Interchange and Neoclassical Metaphysics." *Creative Interchange* edited by John A. Broyer and Wm. S. Minor (Carbondale and Edwardsville: Southern Illonois University Press, 1982): 107-21.

399. "Grounds for Believing in God's Existence." *Meaning, Truth, and God*, ed. Leroy S. Rouner (Notre Dame and London: U of Notre Dame P, 1982): 17-33.

400. Review of Daniel A. Dombrowski. *Plato's Philosophy of History* (Washington, D.C.: UP of America, 1981). *Process Studies* 12, 3 (1982): 201-02.

401. "Anselm and Aristotle's First Law of Modality." *Anselm Studies: An Occasional Journal* 1 (1983): 51-58.

402. Review of George R. Lucas, Jr. *The Genesis of Modern Process Thought: A Historical Outline with Bibliography* (Metuchen, N. J. and London: Scarecrow P, 1983). *Process Studies* 13, 2 (1983): 176-79.

403. "Categories, Transcendentals, and Creative Experiencing." *The Monist* 66, 3 (1983): 319-35.

404. "Peirce's Fresh Look at Philosophical Problems." *Krisis* 1, 1 (1983): 1-5.

405. "Taking Freedom Seriously." Lowell Lecture, 1983. Cambridge Forum, taped lecture # 471 (June 25, 1983) (3 Church Street, Cambridge, Massachusetts, 02138). Unpublished paper that was also presented as a sermon at the First Unitarian Church in Oklahoma City on February 22, 1981.

406. "God and the Meaning of Life." *On Nature*, ed. Leroy S. Rouner. Boston U Studies in Philosophy and Religion, Vol. 6 (Notre Dame, Indiana: U of Notre Dame P, 1984): 154-68.

407. "Toward a Buddhist-Christian Religion." *Buddhism and American Thinkers*, eds. Kenneth K. Inada and Nolan P. Jacobson (Albany: State U of New York P, 1984): 1-13.

408. "Indeterministic Freedom as Universal Principle." *Journal of Social Philosophy* 15 (1984): 5-11.

409. "Marcel on God and Causality." *The Philosophy of Gabriel Marcel*, eds. Paul Arthur Schilpp and Lewis Edwin Hahn. The Library of Living Philosophers, Vol. 17 (La Salle, Illinois: Open Court, 1984): 353-66.

410. "How I got that way," *Existence and Actuality: Conversations with Charles Hartshorne*, eds. John B. Cobb, Jr., and F. I. Gamwell (Chicago: U of Chicago P, 1984). Responses to: Eugene H. Peter, 12-15; Schubert M. Ogden, 37-42; Richard M. Martin, 66-77; William P. Alston, 98-102; John E. Smith, 109-12; Paul Weiss, 121-29; Manley Thompson, 143-48; John B. Cobb, Jr., 164-66; George Wolf, 184-88.

411. "Whitehead as Central but not Sole Philosopher of Process." *Whitehead und der Prozessbegriff*, eds. Harold Holz and Ernest Wolf-Gazo (Freiburg, Nunchen: Karl Alber, 1984): 34-38. From *Proceedings of the First International Whitehead Symposium*, eds. Harold Holz and Ernest Wolf-Gazo, 1981.

412. Foreword to *Divine Omniscience and Human Freedom: Thomas Aquinas and Charles Hartshorne* by John Moskop (Georgia: Mercer UP, 1984): ix-xi.

413. "Theistic Proofs and Disproofs: The Findlay Paradox." *Studies in the Philosophy of J. N. Findlay*, eds. Robert S. Cohen, Richard M. Martin, and Merold Westphal (Albany: State U of New York P, 1985): 224-34.

414. "Creativity as a Value and Creativity as a Transcendental Category." *Creativity in Art, Religion, and Culture*, ed. Michael H. Mitias ([*Elementa: Schriften Zur Philosophie und Ihrer Problemgeschichte*, ed. Rudolph Berlinger and Wiebke Schrader. Band 42 – 1985] Amsterdam: Rodopi, 1985): 3-11.

415. "A Philosophy of Shared Creative Experience." *American Philosophy: A Historical Anthology*, ed. with commentary, Barbara McKinnon (Albany: State U of New York P, 1985): 414-27. Chapter 1 of *Creative Synthesis*. [cf. items 195, 220, and 221]

416. Foreword to *Charles Hartshorne and the Existence of God* by Donald Wayne

Viney (Albany: State U of New York P, 1985): viii-x.

417. "Process Theology in Historical and Systematic Contexts." *Modern Schoolman* 62, 4 (1985): 221-31.

418. Postscript to *God in Process Thought, A Study in Charles Hartshorne's Concept of God* by Santiago Sia (Dordrecht: Martinus Nijoff Publishing, 1985): 113-23.

419. "Scientific and Religious Aspects of Bioethics." *Theology and Bioethics*, ed. E. E. Schelp (Dordrecht, Boston, Lancaster, Tokyo: D. Reidel Publishing Co., 1985): 27-44.

420. "Our Knowledge of God." *Knowing Religiously*. Boston U Studies in Philosophy and Religion, Vol. 7, ed. Leroy S. Rouner (Notre Dame, Indiana: U of Notre Dame P, 1985): 52-63.

421. "Reeves and Stearns on My Idealism." *American Journal of Theology and Philosophy* 7, 1 (1986): 45-50.

422. "Some Perspectives on Chinese Philosophy." *Journal of Chinese Philosophy* 13 (1986): 267-70. Also published in *Philosophie et Culture* Actes du XVIIe Congrès Mondial de Phillosophie. Édition Montmorency, Montréal, 1988: 249-51.

423. "Metaphysics and the Dual Transcendence of God." *Tulane Studies in Philosophy*, "Hartshorne's Neoclassical Theology," eds. Forrest Wood, Jr. and Michael DeArmey, 34 (1986): 65-72.

424. Review of Stephen Toulmin. *Return to Cosmology* (Berkeley, California: U of California P, 1982). *Philosophy and Rhetoric* 19, 4 (1986): 266-269.

425. "Argument in Metaphysics of Religion." *Process Theology and the Christian Doctrine of God*, ed. Santiago Sia. Special edition of *Word and Spirit, A Monastic Review*, 8 (Petersham, Massachusetts: St. Bede's, Publications, 1986): 44-47.

426. "Wisdom as Moderation: A Philosophy of the Golden Mean." Cambridge Forum, taped lecture # 716 (April 9, 1986) (3 Church Street, Cambridge, Massachusetts, 02138). Chapter 2 of *Wisdom as Moderation* followed by audience discussion.

427. "Some Theological Mistakes and Their Effects on Literature." *Journal of Speculative Philosophy*, New Series 1, 1 (1987): 55-72. Chapter 3 of *Zero Fallacy*.

428. Response to resurrection debate in *Did Jesus Rise From the Dead? The Resurrection Debate, Gary Habermas and Antony G. N. Flew*, ed. Terry L. Miethe (San Francisco: Harper & Row, 1987): 137-42.

429. "Pantheism and Panentheism." *The Encyclopedia of Religion*, Senior Ed., Mircea Eliade (New York: Macmillan Publishing Co.; London: Collier Macmillan, Vol. 11, 1987): 165-71.

430. "Transcendence and Immanence." *The Encyclopedia of Religion*, Senior Ed. Mircea Eliade (New York: Macmillan Publishing Co.; London: Collier Macmillan, Vol. 15, 1987): 16-21.

431. "An Anglo-American Phenomenology: Method and Some Results." *Pragmatism Considers Phenomenology*, eds. R. S. Carrington, Carl Hausman, and T. M. Seebohn (Washington: Center for Advanced Research in Phenomenology and UP of America, 1987): 59-71.

432. "Bergson's Aesthetic Creationism Compared to Whitehead's." *Bergson & Modern Thought: Toward a Unified Science*, eds. A.C. Papanicolaou and Pete A.

Gunter (Chur, Switzerland and New York: Harwood Academic Publishers, 1987): 369-82.

433. "Weiss After Sixty Years." *Creativity and Common Sense: Essays in Honor of Paul Weiss*, ed. Thomas Krettek (Albany: State U of New York P, 1987): 262-69.

434. "Mind and Body: A Special Case of Mind and Mind." *A Process Theory of Medicine: Interdisciplinary Essays*, ed. Marcus Ford (Lewiston, New York: Edwin Mellen P, 1987): 77-88.

435. "A Metaphysics of Universal Freedom." *Faith and Creativity: Essays in Honor of Eugene H. Peters*, eds. George Nordgulen and George W. Shields (St. Louis, Missouri: CBP Press, 1987): 27-40.

436. "Reflecting on the Existence [and] Meaning of God." [Interview with Monty Jones]. *The Austin-American Stateman* (Sunday, Jan. 31, 1988): B8.

437. "Can Peirce's Categories Be Retained?" *Philosophie et Culture*, Actes du XVIIe Congrès Mondial de Philosophie. Montréal: Éditions Montmorency, 1988: 140-42.

438. "Some Principles of Procedure in Metaphysics." *The Nature of Metaphysical Knowledge*, eds. G. F. McLean and Hugo Meynell. International Society for Metaphysics (Lanham, New York: UP of America, 1988): 69-75.

439. "Sankara, Nagarjuna, and Fa Tsang, with some Western Analogues." *Interpreting Across Boundaries: New Essays in Comparative Philosophy*, eds. G. J. Larson and Eliot Deutsch (Princeton, New Jersey: Princeton UP, 1988): 98-115.

440. "In Dispraise of Empiricism." *American Journal of Theology and Philosophy* 10, 2 (1989): 123-26.

441. "A Dual Theory of Theological Analogy." *American Journal of Theology and Philosophy* 10, 3 (1989): 171-78. Also in *God, Values, and Empiricism, Issues in Philosophical Theology*, eds. Creighton Peden and Larry Axel (Macon, Georgia: Mercer UP, 1989): 85-91.

442. "Metaphysical and Empirical Aspects of the Idea of God." *Witness and Existence: Essays in Honor of Schubert M. Ogden*, eds. Philip E. Devenish and George L. Goodwin (Chicago: U of Chicago P, 1989): 177-89.

443. "General Remarks." *Hartshorne, Process Philosophy, and Theology*, eds. Robert Kane and Stephen H. Phillips (Albany: State U of New York P, 1989). Replies to David Griffin, 181-83; Jan Van der Veken, 183-84; Barry Whitney, 184-85; Donald Wayne Viney, 186; Daniel Dombrowski, 186-88, Stephen Phillips, 188-90; Kenneth Ketner, 190-92; Lewis S. Ford, 192-94; Robert Kane, 194-95; Jorge L. Nobo, 195-96.

444. "Von Wright and Hume's Axiom." *The Philosophy of Georg Henrik von Wright*, eds. Paul Arthur Schilpp and Lewis Edwin Hahn. The Library of Living Philosophers, Vol. 19 (La Salle, Illinois: Open Court, 1989): 59-76.

445. Foreword and Postscript to *Benevolent Living: Tracing the Roots of Motivation to God* by Richard Hazelett and Dean Turner (Pasadena: Hope Publishing House, 1990): xi-xiv; 313-17.

446. "Charles Hartshorne on Metaphilosophy, Person and Immortality, and Other Issues." An interview with Charles Hartshorne by John Kennedy and Piotr Gutowski [on May 20-21, 1989]. *Process Studies* 19, 4 (1990): 256-78.

447. Review of *The Philosophical Theology of Jonathan Edwards* by Sang Hyun Lee (Princeton: Princeton UP, 1988). *Transactions of the Charles S. Peirce Society* 26, 2 (1990): 249-52.

448. "Response to Piotr Gutowski's 'Charles Hartshorne's Rationalism'." *Process Studies* 19, 1 (1990): 10-14.

449. "Hegel, Logic, and Metaphysics." *CLIO* 19, 4 (1990): 347-52.

450. Critical Response by Charles Hartshorne. *Charles Hartshorne's Concept of God, Philosophical and Theological Responses*, ed. Santiago Sia (Hingam, Massachusetts: Kluwer Publishers, 1990): 241-321. Responses to: [Theodore] Walker on Afro-American and African Theology, 241-42; [Peter] Phan on Liberation Theology, 243-50; [Randall] Morris on Political Philosophy, 251-55; [Sheila Greeve] Devaney on God, Power, and Liberation, 256-62; Arabindu Basu on Indian Thought, 263-65; [Fr. Joseph] Bracken on the God-world Issue, 266-68; [Fr. W. Norris] Clarke's Thomistic Critique, 269-79; [André] Cloots and [Jan] Van der Veken on Panentheism, 280-83; [Hiroshi] Endo's Comparative Study, 284-89; [Piotr] Gutowski on Philosophical Theology, 290-93; [John S.] Ishihara on Buddhism, 294-98; [Rabbi William] Kaufman on Judaism's Idea of God, 299-303; [Martin] McNamara on Biblical Theology, 304-09; [David] Pailin on Rigor, Reason, and Moderation, 310-20; Concluding Remarks [in appreciation of Santiago Sia and the contributors], 320-21.

451. "An Open Letter to Carl Sagan." *The Journal of Speculative Philosophy*, 5, 4 (1991): 227-32.

452. "Communication from Charles Hartshorne" [concerning the history of the Central Division of the American Philosophical Association]. *Proceedings and Addresses of the American Philosophical Association* 65, 3 (1991): 69-70.

453. "Some Causes of My Intellectual Growth." *The Philosophy of Charles Hartshorne*, ed. Lewis Edwin Hahn. The Library of Living Philosophers, Vol. 20 (La Salle, Illinois: Open Court, 1991): 3-45. "A Reply to My Critics," 569-731: Preliminaries and Principles: Reply to Everybody, 569-89; [Charles L.] Birch on Darwin, Chance, and Purpose, 584-86; [Alexander K.] Skutch on Bird Song and Philosophy, 586-89; [Lucio] Chiaraviglio on Song, Evolution, and Theism, 589-98; [Wayne] Viney on Psychology of Sensation, 598-600; [John] Hospers on the Aesthetics of Sensation, 600-06; [Robert] Kane on Freedom and Sufficient Reason, 606-13; Englehardt on Theism and Bioethics, 613-14; [John B.] Cobb [Jr.] on My Theology, 614-16; [William L.] Reese on Panentheism and God's Goodness, 616-17; [Jan] Van der Veken on God and the Ultimate, 617-19; [Jacquelyn Ann] Kegley on Royce and Community, 620-23; [Sallie B.] King on Buddhism, Hierarchy, and Reason, 624-27; [John G.] Arapura on My Response to Vedantism, 627-30; [James P.] Devlin on Metaphysical Asymmetry, 630-33; [Nancy] Frankenberry on Method in Metaphysics, 633-39; [Lewis S.] Ford on Whitehead's and My Philosophy, 640-56; [Norman M.] Martin on the Logic of My Metaphysics, 656-64; [Hubertus G.] Hubbeling on the Ontological Argument, 664-69; [Robert C.] Neville on Temporality and God, 669-72; [T. L. S.] Sprigge on Past, Future, and Eternity, 672-80; [Paul G.] Kuntz on Order and Orderliness, 680-84; [Sterling M.] McMurrin on Neoclassical Metaphysics, 684-88; [Reiner] Wiehl on Whitehead's and My Psychicalism, 688-702; [Daniel A.] Dombrowski on My Platonism, 703-04; [John E.] Smith on the History

of Philosophy, 704-12; [George R.] Lucas [Jr.] on Sources of Process Philosophy, 712-14; Donald Lee on My Pragmatism, 714-21; [Matao] Noda on My Atomism, 721-26; [Keiji] Matsunobu on Philosophy in the Kyoto School, 726-31.

454. "The Aesthetic Dimensions of Religious Experience." *Logic, God and Metaphysics*, ed. J. F. Harris (Dordrecht: Kluwer Academic Publishers, 1992): 9-18.

455. "Some Not Ungrateful But Perhaps Inadequate Comments About Comments on My Writings and Ideas." *Process Studies* 21, 2 (1992): 123-29.

456. "Some Comments on Randall Morris' *Process Philosophy and Political Ideology*." *Process Studies* 21, 3 (1992): 149-51.

457. "Some Under- and Over-rated Great Philosophers [Plato, Bergson, Aristotle, Kant, and others]." *Process Studies* 21, 3 (1992): 166-74.

458. "Hartshorne's Response [to D. Haugen and L. G. Keeling's 'Hartshorne's Process Theism and Big Bang Cosmology']." *Process Studies* 22, 3 (1993): 172.

459. "Can Philosophers Cooperate Intellectually: Metaphysics as Applied Mathematics." *The Midwest Quarterly* 35, 1 (1993): 8-20.

460. "Reminiscences of Charles Hartshorne (member since 1942)." *Journal of Aesthetics and Art Criticism* 51 (1993): 286-89.

461. "God, Necessary and Contingent; World, Contingent and Necessary; and the Fifteen Other Options in Thinking about God: Necessity and Contingency as Applied to God and the World." *Metaphysics as Foundation: Essays in Honor of Ivor Leclerc*, eds. Paul A. Bogaard and Gordan Treash (Albany: State U of New York P, 1993): 296-311.

462. "Interview with Hartshorne, December 1, 1993" (with Randall Auxier). *Hartshorne and Brightman on God, Process, and Persons: The Correspondence, 1922-1945*, eds. Randall E. Auxier and Mark Y. A. Davies (Nashville: Vanderbilt UP, 2001): 88-99.

463. "Three Important Scientists on Mind, Matter, and the Metaphysics of Religion." *The Journal of Speculative Philosophy* 8, 3 (1994): 211-27.

464. "Buddhism and the Theistic Question." *Buddhism and the Emerging World Civilization: Essays in Honor of Nolan Pliny Jacobson*, eds. Ramakrishna Puligandla and David Lee Miller (Carbondale, Illinois: Southern Illinois UP, 1994): 62-72.

465. "Peirce's Philosophy on Religion: Between Two Forms of Religious Belief." *Peirce and Contemporary Thought: Philosophical Inquiries*, ed. Denneth Laine Ketner (New York: Fordham UP, 1995): 339-55.

466. "Freedom as Universal." *Process Studies* 25 (1996): 1-9.

467. "The Meaning of Life." *Process Studies* 25 (1996): 10-18.

468. "Reminiscences of Charles Hartshorne" (excerpted from an unpublished paper: "Importance, Families, Religions, Darwin: A Case Study From the Inside," written in 1994). *Process Perspectives* 20, 3. *Newsletter of the Center for Process Studies*, Special Hartshorne edition (Spring 1997): 8-11.

469. "A Philosopher at 99." [Interview by Steven Vita]. *Austin American Statesman*. (Sunday, April 13, 1997): D1, D7.

470. "A hundred years of thinking about God: a philosopher soon to be rediscovered." [Interview by Greg Easterbrook]. *US News and World Report* (Feb. 23, 1998): 61, 65.

471. "Philosophy (at) 101: Centenarian Charles Hartshorne is Austin's Preeminent Man of Ideas." [Interview by Dayna Finet]. *The Good Life* [published in Austin, Texas] (Oct. 1998): 15-18.

472. "Twenty Opinions from Five Times Twenty Years." *The Personalist Forum*, Special Issue: The Hartshorne Centennial Conference, 14, 2 (1998): 75-76.

473. "Thoughts on the Development of My Concept of God." *The Personalist Forum*, Special Issue: The Hartshorne Centennial Conference, 14, 2 (1998): 77-82.

474. "Charles Hartshorne's Letters to a Young Philosopher: 1979-1995." Ed. Donald Wayne Viney. *Logos-Sophia* [Journal of the Pittsburg State U Philosophical Society, Pittsburg, Kansas] 11 (Fall 2001).

475. "A Psychologist's Philosophy Evaluated After Fifty Years: Troland's Psychical Monism." Ed. Donald Wayne Viney. *Process Studies* 30, 2 (2001): 237-41.

476. "God as Composer-Director and Enjoyer, and in a Sense Player, of the Cosmic Drama." Ed. Donald Wayne Viney. *Process Studies* 30, 2 (2001): 242-53.

477. Audience Discussion of "God as Composer-Director and Enjoyer, and in a Sense Player, of the Cosmic Drama" [April 7, 1987, Central State U, Edmond, Oklahoma]. Ed. Donald Wayne Viney. *Process Studies* 30, 2 (2001): 254-60.

478. "Thomas Aquinas and Three Poets Who Do Not Agree With Him." Ed. Donald Wayne Viney. *Process Studies* 30, 2 (2001): 261-75.

479. "Darwin and Some Philosophers [Review of *Charles Darwin: A New Life* by John Bowlby]." Ed. Donald Wayne Viney. *Process Studies* 30, 2 (2001): 276-88.

480. "Charles Hartshorne's Handwritten Notes on A. N. Whitehead's Harvard-Lecutres 1925-1926." Ed. Roland Faber. *Process Studies* 30, 2 (2001): 289-73.

481. "God, Nature, and Freedom." *God, Nature, and Process Thought: Essays on the Philosophy and Theology of Charles Hartshorne*, ed. Tomasz Komendzinski. (forthcoming). In the same volume, "Response to Zycinski" [Zycinski's article "How to Naturalize Natural Theology?"] and "Response to Pailin." [Pailin's "God as Ultimate, Perfect and Personal"]

482. *Process Theories: Crossdisciplinary Studies in Dynamic Categories.* Dordrecht: Kluwer Academic Publishers, 2003. ed. Seibt, Johanna.

Notes

1. The following items, listed separately in the LLP bibliography, are consolidated under other item numbers in this bibliography; the LLP numbers for these items are: 51, 53, 73, 79, 80, 92, 124, 126, 140, 142, 143, 161, 187, 198, 213, 214, 233, 241, 252, 293, 299, 307, 313, 318, 330, 331, 336, 340, 348, 358, 364, 375, 376, 377, 390, 391, 403, 404, 405, 406, 421, 432, 437, 439, 443, 472, 475, 478.

2. There are 52 items listed in this bibliography that are not in the LLP bibliography. *Books*: 22-25; *Articles, Reviews, Discussions*: 38, 41, 301, 372, 380, 402, 405, 412, 416, 418, 426, 428, 431, 436, 437, 445, 446, 448-452, 454-460, 462, 463, 464, 466-481.